Victory
at the
Gates

Victory at the Gates

By Apostle Vance D. Russell

Published by:
Intermedia Publishing Group
P.O. Box 2825
Peoria, Arizona 85380
www.intermediapub.com

ISBN # 978-0-9819682-0-9

© 2009 Vance D. Russell

Unless otherwise noted, Scripture is taken from the Holy Bible, New International Version, Copyright © 1973, 1978, 1984 by International Bible Society. Used by permission of Zondervan Publishing House. All rights reserved.

Printed in the United States of America by Epic Print Solutions

No part of this publication may be reproduced, stored in a retrieval system, or transmitted in any form or by any means – electronic, mechanical, digital photocopy, recording, or any other without the prior permission of the author.

Victory at the Gates

"Your kingdom come, Your will be done!"

By Apostle Vance D. Russell

Senior Pastor of Arise Ministries International

Austin and San Antonio, Texas

"Lift up your heads, O you gates; be lifted up, you ancient doors that the King of glory may come in. Who is the King of glory? The Lord strong and mighty, the Lord mighty in battle. Lift up your heads, O you gates; lift them up, you ancient doors that the King of glory may come in. Who is he, this King of glory? The Lord Almighty – he is the King of glory (Psalm 24:7-9)!"

About the Author

Apostle Vance D. Russell

Vance is an apostle/prophet with the heart of a visionary and a spiritual father to many. He has served as senior pastor of Arise Ministries International, a church in Austin, Texas for sixteen years. Vance is ordained through Christian International under the authority of Dr. Bill Hamon and is a member of the International Coalition of Apostles (ICA) under the leadership of Dr. Peter Wagner.

Through partnership with the Holy Spirit, he has produced a Christ-centered community. He has established a ministry in San Antonio, Texas where he has planted a church and provides spiritual covering for Arise Metropolitan Assembly in London, England. He is also the spiritual covering for Kingdom Prayer Network an international intercessory network purposed to connect intercessors worldwide. Through Vance's apostolic and prophetic insight many are receiving healing and direction for their lives.

He is an advocate for those who are spiritually seeking a

deeper and more personal relationship with the Lord opening the way for the leading of the Holy Spirit. As a result, he is experiencing miracles, signs and wonders and those who have known only darkness are being set free and are experiencing great joy!

Vance is married to Debbie, his wife of thirty-six years, who he regularly describes as, "His best friend." They have two children, a son Ryan and a daughter Dana, who serve with their parents in the ministry. To his delight, they have an adorable grandson, Noah Andrew.

Foreword

Apostle Vance Russell has received some divine insight concerning the gates. God gives much emphasis to gates in the Bible. This book *Victory at the Gates* will bring much truth to the reader. I have known Vance for many years. He is a minister that has great integrity, honesty and a love for the truth that helps one trust the accuracy of his biblical revelation and application. His statistics and historical information have been thoroughly researched and verified.

I was greatly blessed while reading the manuscript. Every child of God desiring to know truth that can transform their life needs to read this book. Not only does it contain truths that can bless one personally but truth that can enlighten and enable one for transforming society. Vance seeks to reestablish the church back on a true biblical foundation and demonstrate the kingdom of God to the world. There are so many truths and illustrations presented that the only way one can receive the full blessing is to read the book.

The church has moved into its third reformation with God's purpose of demonstrating His Kingdom and the Lordship of Jesus Christ to the world. The living workable realities presented will enlighten and enable those who read to increase their faith to a level they have never been before. God bless you Apostle Vance Russell for blessing the Body of Christ with this tremendous work. May the Holy Spirit cause it to be distributed worldwide so that all Christians may have an opportunity to be blessed by it!

Dr. Bill Hamon
Bishop of Christian International Ministries Network (CIMN)
Author of *The Eternal Church, Day of the Saints*, and many other major books.

Endorsements

"I recently got a chance to preview Apostle Vance Russell's new book, *Victory at the Gates*, and it immediately impacted me. Apostle Vance goes beyond the place where most commentators stop when they write about the decline of Christian influence. He offers a fresh scriptural, apostolic and prophetic insight for ordering your personal life and your calling for maximum impact in High Places. Apostle Vance will lift you into a perspective where you will have a fresh strategy to occupy your gates in the spirit and in the natural. An important book."

Dr. Lance Wallnau
The Lance Learning Group

"As I reviewed this book I realized that it has a legacy anointing upon it. The Hebraic understandings connect us with our history and the rule with Christ Jesus at the gates today. I believe it will be used by many as a reference tool for occupying the gates in their personal life as well as affecting culture. There is a timely progressive journey within the pages that will help bring our lives in alignment with God. Vance has not given us a Bible study alone, but an apostolic prophetic perspective also."

Dr. Sharon Stone
Christian International ~ Europe

"Apostle Vance Russell is a true servant leader who personally models and exemplifies what he teaches and preaches to others and is held in high esteem and utmost respect by those who know him. He is a man of keen revelation and discernment, genuine humility, strong courage and hunger, deep passion and intimacy with the Holy Spirit, personal integrity, and vibrant faith. He is a military strategist and general in the Lord's army and I am privileged and honored to call him friend.

Victory at the Gates provides a critical missing link in the body of knowledge for the church as well as a bridge and framework to connect and integrate the teachings on transforming the Seven Mountains of Society with the rich Hebraic heritage and culture of the twelve spiritual gates which correspond to the twelve months of the year.

This book is simple yet profound, and loaded with fresh insight and revelation from Scripture and the throne of God. *Victory at the Gates* is a must-have for leaders and libraries and will make a great gift for friends and family."

Dr. Bruce Cook
General Partner, Kingdom Venture Partners, LP
Founder of K.E.Y.S. (Kingdom Economic Yearly Summit)

Acknowledgements

I want to first thank the Holy Spirit for guiding my steps on the revelatory journey to discover the twelve spiritual gates, it has literally transformed my life. My heart is filled with love and appreciation for Debbie, my dearest friend and wife of thirty six years. You faithfully listened to my endless conversations about the gates, then supported my efforts by using your notorious red pen and a Thesaurus, I love you sweetie! My respect and love to Prophet Bill Lackie, who released a powerful prophetic word to me about the twelve gates, you are a true friend! I also want to express my gratitude to David Gaddy and Pat Jones for assisting in fine-tuning the verbiage of this book so that all could grasp, in layman's language, this revelation. I would like to acknowledge Eyecue Design, David Gaddy's company, for the images that were provided for each chapter. Many thanks to Dr. Bruce Cook for reading this book twice and lending his expertise and prophetic insight, my friend you really emboldened me to persevere! My highest regard and love to Dr. Bill Hamon, a theologian and my spiritual covering, thank you Bishop for reading and critiquing this material assuring that I did not get off course. Also thanks for writing the foreword and advising me countless times on what to do next, without your guidance I would still be looking for answers. Thank you Rabbi Moshe Genuth, a Torah scholar, philosopher and historian of science for confirming that indeed there is a connection between the Jewish tribes and the months and for establishing the proper use of the senses as they correlate to the tribes. Information from his website, www.inner.org has proven to be an invaluable tool for further discovery of the tribes and their corresponding months. Thank you Arise elders, David and Jayne Gaddy, Mike Wall, Pat and Peggy Williams, Terry and Pat Jones, Betty Lewis, Gaius and Andrea Cameron and Debbie Lewis for being an unbiased sounding board! I am grateful for you and do not take for granted the impact you have individually made in my life. You are the best leadership team ever! To my personal assistant, Jennifer Sheavly, who has maintained her enthusiasm, patience and grace throughout this long process. Words could never express my gratitude for your commitment in partnering to fulfill this assignment. Blessings and love to you, Jen! To our children, Ryan and Dana, and grandson, Noah who fill me with joy and laughter – you keep me smiling. Special thanks to Melissa Adams, Marilyn Jackson, Helen Coffman, Dr. Jim Davis, Apostle Mickey and Prophetess Sandie Freed for their encouragement to continue writing *Victory at the Gates* because, in their words, "This is revelation from God and the Body of Christ needs this!"

Table of Contents

Introduction 1

Chapter 1 ~ The Counterfeit 3

Chapter 2 ~ Who's In Charge 9

Chapter 3 ~ Our Weapons of War 17

Chapter 4 ~ Taking the High Places 23

Chapter 5 ~ Introduction to the Gates 29

Chapter 6 ~ The Gate of Praise 35

Chapter 7 ~ The Gate of Revelation 47

Chapter 8 ~ The Gate of Abundance 57

Chapter 9 ~ The Gate of Righteousness 69

Chapter 10 ~ The Gate of Wisdom 81

Chapter 11 ~ The Gate of Repentance 93

Chapter 12 ~ The Gate of New Beginnings 107

Chapter 13 ~ The Gate of Deliverance 125

Chapter 14 ~ The Gate of Faithfulness 139

Chapter 15 ~ The Gate of Spiritual Maturity 151

Chapter 16 ~ The Gate of Fruitfulness 165

Chapter 17 ~ The Gate of Joy 177

Chapter 18 ~ The Gate of Transformation 191

Epilogue 203

Introduction

A prophet, during one of our church services stopped, in the midst of his ministry, and said these seven words; "*Vance, rule the Twelve Gates of Austin.*" As I prayed and thought about this, I was fascinated at how important it felt to me and no matter what I couldn't get away from it. My attention was drawn to the phrase "*to rule,*" and I asked myself exactly what that really meant? I looked up "rule" in my reference dictionary to verify that it meant to control or direct, to exercise dominating power, authority, or influence over. So not only did I feel that the Lord was asking me to partner with Him regarding the twelve gates of Austin, He was instructing me to rule or govern them in my heart. To govern means to rule over by right of authority, to exercise a directing or restraining influence over. Therefore, we must allow God's presence within us to transform the way we think, speak and act, thereby changing the way we conceive of and interact with the world around us. In other words, in order to see our environment change, first we have to change.

Before going further, I asked for input from several trusted colleagues and theologians, who promptly affirmed that what had been revealed prophetically was indeed revelation from the Lord and needed further investigation and study.

As I read Revelation 21:10-12, I discovered that there were twelve gates with the names of the twelve tribes of Israel written over them. I felt that, this scripture was pivotal and foundational for what the Lord was saying to me. The Lord then impressed upon me that, *if His Church would unite and pray, oiling the hinges and locks of the gates with their tears, He would respond by releasing His presence through them!*

As I continued to pray and study everything I could get my hands on, I was reminded of a scripture that I had read many times before, but this time it grabbed my attention. The scripture was Matthew 6:10, "*…Your kingdom come, your will be done on earth as it is in heaven…*" There was something in this verse that crystallized the overall picture of these twelve gates, specifically that whatever principles govern God's Kingdom (His sphere of power and influence), are also governing earth!

The Lord kept impressing me to focus on governing, and in particular, that from the beginning of creation, His intention was that man rule over the earth (Genesis 1:26-27). My search for the fullness of this revelation focused on the fact that not only is God ruling from heaven, He wants man to rule according to His precepts. I continued to think about the statement, "Rule the twelve gates." I knew that the Holy Spirit had revealed something of crucial importance and that was, *the twelve gates are places where God's people rule spiritually!* Again, in order to see our environment change, first we have to change. Furthermore, we must be alert and train ourselves to be watchmen at these gates, so the counterfeit government established by satan is overthrown, once and for all!

Chapter One

The Counterfeit

"Then I (Nehemiah) said to them, "You see the trouble we are in: Jerusalem (our cities) lies in ruins, and its gates have been burned with fire. Come, let us rebuild the wall of Jerusalem (our cities), and <u>we will no longer be in disgrace</u>."
~ Nehemiah 2:17

I want victory! I want victory for my family, for each member of my ministry and for my city and nation - I want victory for the Body of Christ! I believe you want it too! But how do we achieve it? Through fresh revelation about strategies the Lord gave man long ago! You have no doubt heard people refer to gates before; it is a great metaphor for crossing over from one place to another, but in the book of Revelation, John is shown the New Jerusalem and its twelve gates:

"*And he carried me away in the Spirit to a mountain great and high, and showed me the Holy City, Jerusalem coming down out of heaven from God. It shone with the glory of God, and its brilliance was like that of a precious jewel, like a jasper, clear as crystal. It had a* *great, high wall with twelve gates and with twelve angels at the gates. <u>On the gates were written the names of the twelve tribes of Israel</u>..."* (Revelation 21:10-14).

It is fresh revelation about these gates that the Lord is giving us now that will change the way we pray, the way we do spiritual warfare and the way we live. So, why should you care about the gates? Because this revelation strategy will personally free you and your city of the false counterfeit rule. Satan is a deceiver and desires to overthrow the Body of Christ.

How has satan deceived us and what does it mean?

What would you say if I told you that for generations we have been governed by a counterfeit system set up with the purpose to deceive! Does your mind go immediately to some of the governments in power? Are you inclined to point fingers at outside circumstances that you can't seem to control? I propose that there is sinister intent behind what we see happening that is purposed to steal, kill and destroy!

Let's look at some statistics that will help us understand just how badly we are being impacted by this counterfeit system. This information will propel us to establish the gates as a prayer strategy, targeting specific areas of spiritual need in our world.

- 65 percent of Builders (born from 1910 to 1946) are evangelical
- 35 percent of Boomers (born from 1946 to 1964) are evangelical
- 15 percent of Busters (born from 1965 to 1976) are evangelical
- 4 percent (projected) of Bridger's (born after 1977), AKA Millennial's, will be evangelical (The Bridger Generation, by Thom S. Rainer)

These statistics are sobering and highlight a growing trend among Americans, and especially younger people, who have become progressively more secular in their beliefs, even believing that God, His Word and principles, are no longer relevant. This is humanism. Humanism is defined as a method or system of thinking that is focused on, living one's life aspiring to bring out the finest in mankind so that all people can presumably have the best life possible (be happy). There is nothing inherently wrong with the desire to experience happiness and fulfillment. It's even written in our Constitution in the Bill of Rights. However, the pursuit of happiness, as the driving force of one's life, will leave one feeling empty, dissatisfied and unfulfilled. For proof, just read Ecclesiastes and study the life of Solomon, who denied himself no pleasure under the sun. His conclusion? Vanity, vanity! That is because man was never intended to be the center of the universe. That role and place of honor is reserved for God.

Our nation has a proud heritage of being founded on Judeo-Christian principles. We have enjoyed a society in which the precepts of Scripture have provided moral and ethical governance for our lives. However, as a greater percentage of the populace has ceased to hold core biblical values, our moral standards have declined and there is no longer a potent majority who screams loudly when these principles are violated.

But it gets worse; our culture has abandoned moral ethics. Currently, every second, 44,444 users are viewing a pornographic website. Pornography is justified by some to be a way of breaking out of the narrow confines of "uptight" morality to discover one's true sexually liberated self. This thought has fueled the explosion of pornography in our society.

The impact of the perversion that many of our fathers and mothers (Builders and Boomers) have set in motion is seen in the 2008 statistics where nearly 3 million teenagers in the U.S. have become infected with Sexually Transmitted Diseases (STD). In 2007, some 750,000 U.S. teens became pregnant and at least one in four had a sexually transmitted disease. The most recent figures released from the National Center for Disease Control (NCDC) states that the incidence of teen suicide rose from 6400 suicides per 100,000 adolescent deaths to 9400 in 2007. <u>Every day</u>, on average, 11,318 American youth ages 12 to 20 try alcohol for the first time. Nearly one third reported hazardous drinking (five or more drinks in one setting) during the 30 days preceding this survey (www.TheMarioninstitute.org/youth/alcohol-youth.htm). In fact, our children often reflect the values and behaviors of their parents!

Pollster George Barna reported that 83 percent of teenagers in the U.S. believe that *"moral absolutes depend on the circumstances."* What we do in the next five to seven years will affect this country for the next several generations. Every year in America over four million teens turn 20 years old. The report affirms that by the time a person reaches 20, the odds of reaching them for Christ are 10 to 1! What we believe at 13, we will die believing unless God intervenes. Faced with this evidence, what will our society look like in ten years? What percentage of our marriages will stay together? Where will this new generation take us? What sort of world will our children and grandchildren grow up in? Will we be guilty of allowing ourselves to be the last generation in America that had the benefit of strong Christian ethics in our moral values and legal codes?

Now, sit back for a moment, take a deep breath and think about what you have just read. Invite the Holy Spirit to stir within you the passion to reform what you have accepted as a way of life. We have the opportunity to change this situation; the Holy Spirit will help us! Only the Lord can alter our circumstances, as we permit Him to transform us.

Allow me to continue. In his book, *Absolute Confusion*, Barna says, "From a biblical perspective, the profile that emerges as we take a glimpse of theology in America is *frightening*. The lack of accurate knowledge <u>about</u> God's Word, His principles for life, and the apparent absence of influence the church has upon the thinking and behavior of this nation is a rude awakening for those who assume we are in the midst of a spiritual revival." The point of encouragement is that we have nearly unrestricted opportunities to analyze the spiritual needs through these and many other bright spots so that we can change a confused culture in powerful ways. "<u>But time is of the essence</u>!"

"We are challenged, however, to help people understand Christianity in a way that differentiates it from all other religious systems. *The Christians they meet act no different from other people.* The churches they pass on the way to work have little presence in the community and appear to do little apart from their Sunday morning rituals."

"Somehow, many Americans have heard, and accepted the notion, that a fellow named Jesus Christ once lived and did some rather unusual things, but the connection between those events and their own lives is missing. Even their view of God has frequently remained untainted by the teachings of the Bible. Until we get our own House of Faith in order, the chance of us leaving a lasting, life changing impression on outsiders is negligible."

"In short, the spirituality of Americans is Christian in name only. We desire experience more than knowledge. We prefer choice to absolutes. We embrace preferences rather than truths. We seek comfort rather than growth. Faith must come on our terms or we reject it. We have enthroned ourselves as the final arbiters of righteousness, the ultimate rulers of our own experience and destiny. We have become, …*Pharisees of the new millennium*!"

What we see in part is the fruit of a counterfeit system that we have allowed to be established, dismantling the foundation on which God intended us to build our lives. This is leading us in a direction that serves only to diminish what it means to be sons and daughters of God. Let us allow the Holy Spirit to open our eyes to any way that we have surrendered our spiritual identity and laid down God's divine purposes. The Lord wants us to connect with His Kingdom and overthrow the imposter determined to tear apart and destroy any semblance of God's Kingdom!

Chapter Two

Who's in Charge?

"<u>Pass through, pass through the gates</u>! Prepare the way for the people. Build up, build up the highway! Remove the stones (demonic foundations). Raise a banner for the nations. The Lord has made proclamation to the ends of the earth: "Say to the Daughter of Zion (Church), 'See, his reward is with him, and his recompense accompanies him.'" They will be called the Holy People, the redeemed of the Lord; and you will be called Sought After, <u>the City No Longer Deserted</u>."
~ Isaiah 62:10-12

It is obvious we have been deceived! There is an imposter sitting at the threshold of the gates of our lives and cities and he is trying to determine what enters and departs. We have personally experienced the consequences of being governed by these frauds. The question is who will replace these counterfeit agents? As it turns out scripture is very clear on who God intends to be the administrators of His government. From Genesis through Revelation we see God fully intending that His sons and daughters rule! Some of you may feel that salvation is all that the Lord has purposed for us. However, there is a greater plan that God longs for us to partner with and that is to establish His Kingdom on earth and rule with Him. There is *Victory at the Gates*!

What is the importance of the gates and why should we care?

During the course of my study, I found that historically, gates served as entrances and exits of a city. They were places where business (II Kings 7:10), legal transactions (Ruth 4:1-11), and public discourse (II Samuel 19:8) occurred. Gates were opened during the day to allow citizens to come and go, and were closed at night for safety. Because of their central location, they are referenced, many times, as, <u>symbols of power and authority</u>. I also found several examples of gates being used for spiritual activity (I Kings 22:10; Ezekiel 11:1). I asked the Lord, how does this relate to governing the gates of my heart and my city? He directed me to *Revelation 21:10-14*, which says, *"And he carried me away in the Spirit to a mountain great and high, and showed me the Holy City, Jerusalem coming down out of heaven from God. It shone with the glory of God, and its brilliance was like that of a precious jewel, like a jasper, clear as crystal. It had a great, high wall with twelve gates and with twelve angels at the gates. <u>On the gates were written the names of the twelve tribes of Israel</u>..."* From this point on, when we use the term gate or twelve gates I will be referring to "<u>The New Jerusalem Gates on earth</u>."

As I considered Revelation 21:12, I was reminded of the statement, *"nothing happens in the natural that first did not occur in God's Kingdom."* Two examples are Adam and Jesus. Adam was conceived in God's heart before the Lord created him: *"Then God said, "Let us make man in our image, in our likeness, and let them rule over the fish of the sea and the birds of the air, <u>over all the earth</u>, and over all the creatures that move along the ground.* The prophetic word became reality when, *"…God created man in his own image, in the image of God he created him; male and female he created them"* (Genesis 1:27). Then Isaiah 7:14 refers to the birth of Jesus, *"Therefore the Lord himself will give you a sign; The virgin will be with child and will give birth to a son, and will call him Immanuel,"* which found its fulfillment in *Matthew 2:1-2, "After Jesus was born in Bethlehem in Judea, during the time of King Herod, Magi from the east came to Jerusalem and asked, "Where is the one who has been born king of the Jews? We saw his star in the east and have come to worship him."*

More importantly, Genesis 1:26 identifies the purpose for the creation of man. God's intention for man was to govern His creation. Frank E. Gaebelein, in his *Expositors Bible Commentary*, says, "Only man has been given dominion (supreme power or control) in God's creation. This dominion is expressly stated to be over all other living creatures, sky, sea, land creatures and over all the earth. If we ask why the author of Genesis has singled out the creation of man this way, one obvious answer is that he intended to portray him (man) as a special creature, marked off from the rest of God's work. Man is a special creature, he's made in the image and likeness of God," and <u>so we must rule and reign as our Father does</u>!

<u>What does it mean to govern and what are the functions of the gates?</u>

Because we have been commissioned to govern according

to Genesis 1:26, we have to ask ourselves what does governing look like and what role do the gates play? Jesus said in Matthew 6:10, "...*Your kingdom come, your will be done on earth as it is in heaven*." We're not only to be governed by this principle, but we're to govern through it. The first step to govern properly is confirmed in Matthew 22:37, "...*'Love the Lord your God with all your heart and with all your soul and with all your (entire) mind.' This is the first and greatest commandment. And the second is like it: 'Love your neighbor as yourself.' All the Law and the Prophets hang on these two commandments.*" We must allow God's principles to govern us so we can govern our situations. This defines what governing looks like.

Secondly, what role do the gates play? To give us a better understanding of what the word "gate" means let's look at several definitions that will give us clarity. In biology a gate is a temporary channel in a cell membrane through which nutrients or waste passes. Using this to shed light on the gates, they become access points by which information, given by God, provides a way for spiritual nourishment and enrichment to flow in and toxins (sin) to flow out.

The word "gate" also describes the way we act, the things we do, or a path which governs the way we live. Taking these definitions into consideration, *gates are openings which serve as conduits for God's Kingdom to touch us changing the way we think, behave and speak*! The word gate is simply a term to describe access points through which the kingdom is conveyed, it also denotes unique ways that heaven connects with you and I. This allows us to focus on what is being expressed rather than how it is being expressed. Gates then, serve as the entrance point for revelation from heaven, which transforms us!

Biblical examples of people governing their situations were demonstrated in the lives of David and Esther. For instance, David was identified by God at a young age and anointed by Samuel to lead God's people into their rightful place. We see during the course of David's life many instances where his leadership was developed, fashioning him into a man who understood what it meant to govern God's chosen people according to His principles. David paid a high price to learn some of these lessons of kingship (I Samuel chapters 16-30; II Samuel chapters 1-2). Another example is how God placed Esther in a position of influence for the purpose of bringing salvation to the Hebrew people who were threatened with certain annihilation (Esther chapters 1-10). In order to overturn the counterfeit system we have allowed to be established, we must permit God's principles to govern us just as David and Esther did. When we do this we will see the enemy dispossessed of his influence! We must take upon ourselves the responsibility to keep the spiritual climate over our lives and cities conducive for God to inhabit and move. This can only be achieved as we die to self, become sensitive to the voice of the Lord, obedient to accomplish His directives and confident that the Spirit of God Himself leads the way!

In order to dislodge the powers of hell over our lives, we must walk in the authority that God has given us! *To be released in this area we first must learn to submit to authority*! This requires that we stop pointing fingers at circumstances and people that surround us causing us to be easily offended and controlled by our feelings and emotions. If we will take responsibility for our lives and support our leadership and one another, incredible results will happen! I believe that God wants us to be released into our authority so that we can become His battle axe to overthrow the counterfeit system that the enemy has established. True authority begins as we learn to serve others; but the greatest act of governing is experienced as we become the servant of all!

A city is a center of population where government, commerce and culture take place. From a kingdom perspective, there are many ways the Lord can carry out His business; I fervently believe one way is through the twelve gates. These gates are not physical places in our cities verified through our five senses; *they are passageways that will have a profound impact on the spiritual climate.* So what role do the gates play? They are venues where we can engage and overthrow our unseen enemies *"For our struggle is not against flesh and blood, but against the rulers, against the authorities, against the powers of this dark world and against the spiritual forces of evil in the heavenly realms" (Ephesians 6:12).*

One place to begin to access the gates is through historical information. For instance, the first month on the Jewish calendar is Nissan and the tribe associated with it is Judah, meaning praise. In II Chronicles 20:22 and Matthew 21:9-13 it confirms that when we praise the Lord it moves Him to do war against the enemies that have aligned themselves against us: *"As they began to <u>sing and praise</u>, the Lord <u>set ambushes</u> against the men of Ammon and Moab and Mount Seir who were invading Judah, and they were <u>defeated</u>" (II Chronicles 20:22).* In the New Testament we also see praise moving the Lord on our behalf. *"The crowds that went ahead of him (Jesus) and those that followed shouted, 'Hosanna* *to the son of David!' 'Blessed is he who comes in the name of the Lord!' 'Hosanna in the highest!' When Jesus entered Jerusalem, the whole city was stirred and asked, 'Who is this?' The crowds answered, this is Jesus, the prophet from Nazareth in Galilee."* Because of their praise *"...Jesus entered the temple area and drove out all who were buying and selling there. He overturned the tables of the moneychangers and the benches of those selling doves. "It is written," he said to them, "'My house shall be called a house of prayer,' but you are making it a 'den of robbers'"* (Matthew 21:9-13). Once again, when you praise the Lord He rises up as a man of war against your enemies.

In reality, the Lord left us in charge to establish His Kingdom on earth but we have unknowingly surrendered that authority to the enemy. As those who have been commissioned to dismantle the high places and called to rule, we must take our rightful position as God's sons and daughters!

Chapter Three

Our Weapons of War

*"The weapons we fight with are not the weapons of this world.
On the contrary, they have divine power to demolish strongholds."*
~ II Corinthians 10:4

You may be saying, well now that's news to me! I'm supposed to be in charge? You're saying that I'm to govern the gates? Oh sure, good thinking! Even if I did agree with this thought, where would I begin? The place to start is to remind ourselves that nothing occurs in the natural without first occurring in the spiritual.

Scripture confirms that there is a kingdom in heaven that is ruled by the Lord (Revelation 21:1-13; Matthew 6:10) and one on earth ruled by satan (Matthew 4:1-11; Luke 11:18). People in the New Testament believed implicitly in evil spirits who filled the air and were determined to cause men harm. The words, *powers, authorities, world rulers,* are all names for different classes of these evil spirits (Ephesians 6:12). Christian's are not only invited to have relationship with the Lord, but in the context of that relationship we are to wage war against the forces that align themselves against the Lord's purposes.

As we position ourselves to overthrow the counterfeit system with spiritual warfare, Paul informs us of the armor that God has made available to us. He takes the armor of the Roman soldiers and translates it into Christian terms. There is the <u>belt of truth</u>, which secures the soldiers tunic (clothing) from binding him and it is also an item from which his sword hung giving freedom of movement. Paul then refers to our <u>breastplate of righteousness</u>, which was designed to protect the heart. Your <u>feet are fitted with the readiness that comes from the gospel of peace</u> giving solid footing for battle. Peace defined is freedom of the mind from annoyances, distractions anxiety and fear. Without peace you will surely fail! Next Paul makes reference to the <u>shield of faith</u>. The word he uses is for the great oblong shield which the heavily armed warrior wore on his arm. One of the most dangerous weapons in ancient warfare was the fiery dart. It was tipped with yarn, dipped in pitch, set on fire and then thrown. The great oblong shield was made of two sections of wood glued together. When it was hit by the dart it sank into the wood and the flame was extinguished. Our faith is much like the shield, when we are hit by the lies of the enemy our faith quickly quenches them. The sixth article worn during battle is the <u>helmet of salvation</u>. Salvation, which is in Christ, gives us forgiveness of sins and shields our minds from being accosted by the enemy. We must put on *"...Faith and love as a breastplate and the hope of salvation as a helmet..."* (I Thessalonians 5:8) if we are to successfully engage our enemy. Finally, there is the <u>sword</u>

which is the Word of God, which can be used as a defensive or offensive weapon. We must learn not to just wait for the enemy to attack; *we must take the battle to the enemy!* Then Paul comes to the greatest weapon of all and that is prayer. <u>Our prayer must be consistent</u>. It is our tendency so often to pray only in the great crisis of life; but it is from daily prayer that the Christian will find their strength. <u>It must be intense</u>. Limp prayer never got a man anywhere; it demands the concentration of every faculty upon God. <u>It must be unselfish</u>. Many of our prayers are centered on us and too little on others! We must learn to pray as much for others as for ourselves.

<u>What does prayer have to do with the gates</u>?

You may not be aware of the need to pray, or you may lack the understanding that aggressive prayer shatters the plans of the enemy. Paul says in II Corinthians 10:3-5, *"For though we live in the world, we do not wage war as the world does. The weapons we fight with are not the weapons of the world; on the contrary, they have a divine power to demolish strongholds. We demolish arguments and every pretention that sets itself up against the knowledge of God, and we take captive every thought to make it obedient to Christ. And we will be ready to punish every act of disobedience, once your obedience is complete."* We will change our environment through strategic prayer as we are transformed into the likeness of Christ. We will never rule the gates of our cities without first allowing the Lord to rule the gates of our hearts.

Intercession means to intervene on behalf of another. It has always been from a heart of love and care for others that intercession is effective. One of the earliest and best examples of intercession occurs in Genesis 18, where Abraham speaks to God on behalf of Sodom. His plea is compassionate; it is concerned with the well-being of others rather than with his own needs. Such selfless concern is the mark of effective intercession. Another good example is the intercessory prayers of Moses. The leader of the nation and a righteous man, Moses successfully petitioned God on behalf of the Hebrew people (Exodus 15:25). Even the Pharaoh asked Moses to intercede for him (Exodus 8:28). But just as righteous people often succeeded in reconciling Creator and creation, the Bible also reminds us that the continued sinful behavior of people can hinder the effects of intercession (I Samuel 2:25; Jeremiah 7:16).

The sacrifice and prayers of Old Testament priests (Exodus 29:42, 30:7) were acts of intercession that point forward to the work of Christ. Jesus is of course, the greatest intercessor who ever lived! He prayed on behalf of Peter (Luke 22:32) and His disciples (John 17). He wept over the City of Jerusalem (Matthew 23:37). Then in the most selfless intercession of all, He petitioned God on behalf of those who crucified Him (Luke 23:34). But Christ's intercessory work did not cease when He returned to heaven. In heaven He continually intercedes for His church from a position of authority at the right hand of God (Hebrews 7:25) and His Holy Spirit pleads on behalf of individual Christians (Romans 8:26-27). Because of their unique relationship to God through Jesus, Christians are charged to intercede for all the people (I Timothy 2:1) and rulers of the earth (Romans 13:1-8).

As you pray, see yourself behind Jesus Christ who goes in front of you and battles against the enemies that have set themselves against you at the gates (Micah 2:12-13; John 10:3-4;

Isaiah 45:1-2). While fear should not drive you, wisdom should, so being strategic about what you pray and decree is extremely important. Furthermore, realize that negotiating with satan only exasperates the situation, since we cannot barter with the enemy by saying, "satan I'll leave you alone, if you'll leave me alone!" It is important that we do battle without voicing something that the enemy can use against us and pray by faith remembering that without it we cannot please the Lord (Hebrews 11:6).

E.M. Bounds speaks of men that moved God by their prayers. John Wesley spent two hours daily in prayer. He began in the morning, and one who knew him wrote: "He thought prayer to be more his business than anything else and I have seen him come out of his closet with a serenity of face next to shining." John Fletcher <u>stained the walls of his room by the breath of his prayers</u>. Sometimes he would pray all night; always, frequently, and with great earnestness. His whole life was a life of prayer. "I would not rise from my seat," he said, "without lifting my heart to God."

David Legge recounts the story of John Hyde of India. Praying Hyde, as he was known, was on the mission field and he stayed there until his health required him to withdraw. Once he returned home, he sought the counsel of a physician. Upon examination the doctor asked him, "Mr. Hyde, do you have any pains in your chest?" He said, "yes I do!" He said, "Mr. Hyde, your heart has displaced itself, it ought to be here, but it's moved over into the cavity of your chest and that can only happen through agony!" He was the apostle of prayer and his prayers led thousands into the kingdom of God and into the church of India.

To see the environment change we must allow the Lord to examine our hearts as we pick up our weapons of spiritual warfare! This is a critical time for our nation, and we must respond to the call petitioning the Lord for His help as we take back the high places in our lives and cities!

Chapter Four

Taking the High Places

"Tear down your father's altar to Baal and cut down the Asherah beside it. Then build a proper kind of altar to the Lord your God on top of this height. Using the wood of the Asherah pole that you cut down, offer the second bull as a burnt offering."
~ Judges 6:25c-26

A king had just won a war, but he knew from experience, that was the easy part. If he wanted to occupy the land that he had just conquered, he needed to win the hearts and minds of the people; these were the real high places. He would have to become an influencer!

Webster's Dictionary defines "High Places," as a place of worship, usually a temple or altars on a hilltop. The *Nelson's New Illustrated Bible Dictionary* says, "Most of the Old Testament references to high places imply a form of pagan worship forbidden to the Israelites." Scripture confirms that in order for the Lord to establish His Kingdom prior to Him moving, He always requires the spiritual environment to be properly aligned and changed. For example, the first act of Gideon, as well as other examples throughout the Bible, required him to remove the high place that was over the area and dethrone false pagan gods and idols (Judges 6:25c-26). We see this cycle continuously throughout Jewish history, in that evil kings came to the throne in Judah and built high places to worship and offer sacrifices, and succeeding <u>good kings</u> abolished them. For instance, during Rehoboam's reign high places appeared (I King 14:23), but Hezekiah broke them down (II Kings 18:4). Wicked Manasseh built them again (II Kings 21:3), but righteous Josiah dismantled them (II Kings 23:8).

<u>*Where are the high places and what do I need to do about them*?</u>

Change must first start with us! Taking this statement into consideration, I asked myself if I had allowed high places to be established in my life. Allow me to share something that had become a high place for me. The Lord revealed that I had permitted rejection to operate in my life. It was easier to reject others before they rejected me. This has been a long process, but through His mercy I am being healed daily! You may find that you have set in order issues that are contrary to God's principles just as I did. For instance, when the Lord wants us to be generous, do we find ourselves governed by feelings of scarcity? When the Lord wants us to show compassion, are we unable to sympathize with others because we are driven by our past hurts? Whatever the issue, if you will surrender your life to the Lord, He will heal you and that is precisely what is needed.

Next, we must look at the high places in the environment around us. It is generally accepted that there are seven spheres of influence, or mountains, governed by people that have authority to shape nations, positively or negatively. These areas are Family, Religion, Education, Media, Arts/Entertainment, Business/Finance and Government. The men and women that rule these areas have the prerogative to establish godly or ungodly principles depending on the spiritual atmosphere that governs them. *The seven spheres in and of themselves are neither good nor bad.* The groups of people that govern them exert influence over our lives and *therein lies the problem*! People that operate within these spheres and those that are affected by them need to experience and embrace God's Kingdom; the twelve gates are one way that this can happen.

What are the Twelve Gates and what do they mean to me?

Through study and prayer I have identified the twelve gates. They are Praise, Revelation, Abundance, Righteousness, Wisdom, Repentance, New Beginnings, Deliverance, Faithfulness, Spiritual Maturity, Fruitfulness, and Joy as well as Transformation during leap year. As these gates are opened in our hearts through our prayers as well as submission to our loving Father, a seismic shift will occur initiating one of two options. Either the people who rule the seven spheres will allow themselves to be governed by the precepts of the kingdom, causing them to think and behave differently, or the Lord will replace them with those who will!

The twelve gates are established in our lives, first, by being aware that they exist, second, by learning how to access the principles of them through prayer, and third, by applying them in our everyday lives. The twelve gates are designed to open heaven's favor over our lives and then our cities! It's only by the Lord's presence saturating His people that we can realize the freedom that's afforded us as children of God!

Romans 12:2 says: "Do not conform any longer to the pattern of this world, but be transformed by the renewing of your mind. Then you will be able to test and approve what God's will is – His good, pleasing and perfect will." The word conformed means to act in accord to prevailing standards. The Apostle Paul is saying, that our conduct must be dictated by God's pattern, meaning don't be like a chameleon that takes its color from its surroundings.

The word Paul uses for "transformed," means that we must undergo a change that affects the way we think and thus the way we behave. This happens through the renewal of our minds. We must walk according to God's pattern and allow the Holy Spirit to govern our hearts, thereby redeeming the high places.

Proverbs 23:7 (KJV) says, *"For as he thinketh in his heart so is he."* J. Oswald Sanders says it like this, *"The mind of man is the battleground on which every moral and spiritual battle is fought."* Our minds are powerful organs created by God and they are shaped by the information that is taken into them. Like a computer we either have good information or bad, "Good in Good out, Garbage in Garbage out!" *In all honesty, your thoughts <u>govern</u> your actions*. In the case of the seven spheres they are governed by *something or someone* who determines their philosophy, which shapes them. The information that is dispersed comes from a source and it must be identified and transformed. When we think about the forces that shape our culture do we view them as something that is outside of ourselves or do we see them as something that we are called to influence through our prayers and actions? Our inclination is to look at things from a clinical perspective and process, gathering information, analyzing data and delivering judgments, without taking personal responsibility. We should ask ourselves, have we become part of the problem, or part of the solution?

So where do we go from here? Rather than blaming our culture for our problems we must take responsibility to govern the environment that is negatively influencing it. As we are faithful to apply the twelve gates to our lives, allowing their principles to transform our thoughts, everything that we touch will emanate God's Kingdom, and we will change the very environment where we live! *The twelve gates then become places where God's people must rule spiritually and as we apply the gates to our lives, we will see the environment around us change!*

Chapter Five

Introduction to the Gates

The following information is designed to provide a context for you to understand as you apply the gates to your life.

- The names of the tribes are taken from Numbers 2:1-30 and according to a Hebrew chart attached on the subsequent page.

- Every tribe is associated with a specific month on the Jewish calendar. For instance, Judah is connected to the month of Nissan and Issachar is joined to the month of Iyar, etc. (Please refer to the diagram of the Hebraic calendar that explains the correlation between each month and the tribes below).

- Here are the names of the months, their connection with the Gregorian calendar and scriptural support.

    1. Nisan – March/April – Exodus 13:4
    2. Iyar (Ziv) – April/May – I Kings 6:1
    3. Sivan – May/June – Esther 8:9
    4. Tammuz – June/July – Jeremiah 39:2; Zechariah 8:19
    5. Av (Ab) – July/August – Numbers 33:38; Zechariah 7:3
    6. Elul – August/September – Nehemiah 6:15
    7. Tishri – September/October – I Kings 8:2
    8. Cheshvan (Bul) – October/November - I Kings 6:38
    9. Kislev – November/December – Ezra 10:9
    10. Tevet – December/January – Esther 2:16

11. Shevat – January/February - Zechariah 1:7
12. Adar – February/March – Esther 3:7
13. Adar II once every three years
    (the Pregnant year) - February - March
    * Refer to page 31, bullet 4

- Unlike our Gregorian calendar, the Jewish calendar is lunisolar for predominately religious purposes. It is intended to align the Jewish New Year and dates for Jewish holidays, as well as daily psalm readings, among many ceremonial uses. The principles of the Hebrew calendar are found in the Torah, which contains several calendar related commandments, including God's commandment during their Exodus from Egypt establishing Nissan as the first month of the year (Exodus 12:2). The Babylonian exile in the 6th century BCE influenced the calendar including the adoption of Babylonian names for the months (obtained from Wikipedia – Jewish calendar).

- The gates are taken from the study of the names of each tribe. For instance, Judah means praise, so the gate name is <u>Praise</u>! Because Judah and Nissan are connected it is during this time that we celebrate by praying that God open the gate of praise in our hearts. The names of the gates indicate ways God shows up and touches us.

- As we study the gates we should expect the Lord to highlight specific areas that need attention in our lives. For instance, in my research about Nissan I found that Israel was delivered from Egypt during this month. Prophetically, I felt that God was inviting me into a time of self examination where He

Introduction to the Gates

would bring to my attention some things that I needed to be delivered from. I encourage each reader to petition the Lord for prophetic insight as you work and pray through each gate.

- Because the beginning and end of the Jewish months change each year please refer to www.hebcal.com so that you're aware of the changes.

- I recommend using the prophetic information as your intercessory points during your prayer time.

- Praying the gates is done on a continual basis as each gate builds on the previous. For instance, the information that was given during the month of Nissan is continued through the month of Iyar and so forth.

- According to Jewish custom the Hebrew calendar is lunisolar which indicates both the moon phase and the time of the solar year with an embolismic or extra month which is referred to as a pregnant year. During the pregnant years of 2003, 6, 8, 11, 14, 17 and 19 this extra month is called Adar Alef, The Gate of Transformation, which precedes Adar. Adar Alef becomes the first Adar and the customary Adar which is the Gate of Joy, becomes Adar Bet meaning the second Adar.

- Although you may feel that this is redundant, remember that the twelve gates are places where God's people rule spiritually. *In order to see the world that we live in change, <u>we have to change</u>!*

The following information is not intended for us to participate or become involved in Jewish festivals or customs. It is designed to enhance our Christian experience. Please see the different Gate names that align with tribes and Hebraic months.

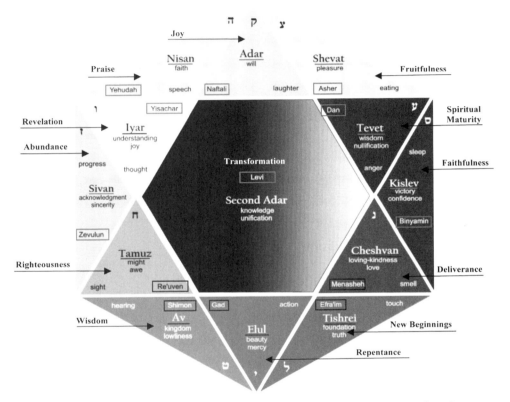

Please read counter clockwise following the months from Nissan the first month to Iyar the second and so forth. Levi is the thirteenth month of the pregnant year and is concurrent with leap year on our Gregorian calendar. You'll find the Color, Letter, Sefirah, Inner Motivator and the Sense included in this chart as well. The Sefirah, Inner Motivator and the sense for each month will be further explained as you study the individual gates. Please find on the next page a table of interpretation that converts Hebrew language into our English definition.

Introduction to the Gates

Spiritual Gates Quick Reference Sheet

Gate	Hebraic Month	Tribe	Length	Gregorian Month
Praise	Nisan	Judah	30 days	March / April
Revelation	Iyar	Issachar	29 days	April / May
Abundance	Sivan	Zebulon	30 days	May / June
Righteousness	Tammuz	Reuben	29 days	June / July
Wisdom	Av	Simeon	30 days	July / August
Repentance	Elul	Gad	29 days	August / Sept.
New Beginnings	Tishri	Ephraim	30 days	Sept. / Oct.
Deliverance	Cheshvan	Manasseh	29 or 30 days	Oct. / Nov.
Faithfulness	Kislev	Benjamin	29 or 30 days	Nov. / Dec.
Spiritual Maturity	Tevet	Dan	29 days	Dec. / Jan.
Fruitfulness	Shevat	Asher	30 days	Jan. / Feb.
Joy	Adar I	Naphtali	30 days	Feb. / March
*Transformation	Adar II (leap)	Levi	29 days	Feb. / March

* For an explanation of the 13th month, The Gate of Transformation, please refer to page 31, bullet 4.

Chapter Six

The Gate of Praise

"Through Jesus, therefore, let us continually offer to God a sacrifice of praise – the fruit of the lips that confess His name."
~ Hebrews 13:15

OVERVIEW

The <u>first month</u> (Exodus 13:4) on the Jewish calendar is "<u>Nissan</u>" and it begins in March and ends in April on the Gregorian calendar. The tribe associated with this month is "<u>Judah</u>" and it means "<u>praise</u>, spring, or a time when life becomes prevalent." The gate name is "The Gate of <u>Praise</u>." The festival that is celebrated during this time is "Passover" and it begins God's yearly cycle. The Feast of Passover is designed to set us on a course that will draw us closer to God and into a fresh experience with His Glory each year.

GENERAL INFORMATION

"Praise" in Scripture means to proclaim the Lord's "merit" or "worth." There are many terms in the Bible used to communicate praise; they include glory, blessing, thanksgiving and the word hallelujah, which in Hebrew means, "Praise the Lord." Also there are various viewpoints and interpretations of the purpose of praise in the Body of Christ. Many perceive it as a time of entertainment with little or no worth. I would like for you to see praise from another dimension, that of an effective weapon of war. Hosea 10:11 says, "…<u>Judah must plow</u> …" In Hebrew, Judah means praise, therefore, praise is designed to plow the hearts of men and women so that they might receive the Word of God.

From a New Testament perspective, Matthew 21:7-9 conveys that the people worshipped Jesus when He came into Jerusalem. Matthew 21:12 says "Jesus entered the temple area and drove out all who were buying and selling there. He turned over the tables of the moneychangers and benches of those selling doves. "It is written," he said to them, "My house will be called a house of prayer, 'but you are making it a 'den of robbers.'" This is a perfect example of the Lord's response when we praise Him. Infused by the atmosphere of praise and worship, Jesus was transformed from the lowly lamb riding on a colt, to the roaring Lion of the Tribe of Judah! <u>Immediately after the people praised Jesus, He went into the Temple and spiritually cleansed it</u>. Another example of praise changing the spiritual atmosphere is found in Isaiah 42:10-13, *"Sing to the Lord a new song, his praise from the ends of the earth, you who go down to the sea, and all that is in it, you islands, and all who live in them. Let the desert and its towns raise their voices; let the settlements where Kedar lives rejoice. Let the people of Sela sing for joy; let them shout from the mountaintops. Let them give glory to the Lord and proclaim his praise in the islands. The Lord will march out like a mighty man, like a warrior he will stir up his zeal; with a shout he will raise the battle cry and will triumph over his enemies."* As in Matthew 21, when praise goes forth, the Lord rises as a mighty man of war and triumphs over His enemies and when you praise Him, your enemies become His enemies. The zeal expressed in Isaiah 42:10-13 is far from the lifeless praise services many churches experience. Other forms of warfare praise that can be used are the <u>clapping of hands</u> (Isaiah 55:12), <u>shouting</u> (Isaiah 12:6; II Samuel 6:14-15), <u>singing</u> (Acts 16:25-26), <u>dancing</u> (Isaiah 30:31-32), and the use of <u>musical instruments</u> (Psalm 144:1).

When we gather corporately we should anticipate the presence of the Lord appearing in our midst. Our hearts should be purposed to magnify Jesus knowing that when we do, He will be unleashed to do war against our enemies. Therefore, praise is an important weapon in the mouth of God's people; it isn't just another religious activity. When you have difficulty hearing the Lord, praise Him! When you need an answer for an issue, praise Him! When you're depressed and despondent, praise Him! Psalm 150 instructs us when we gather in our corporate services to, <u>"Praise the Lord, let everything that has breath, Praise the Lord</u>*!"*

Prophetically

My research revealed that during Nissan, the Lord is breathing upon you. The Hebrew word "Hei" means the window of God's breath blowing down on you and is prevalent during this time. It's known as the month of wind, for instance tornados and hurricane winds may occur. It should be emphasized that where these winds appear, you should look intently to that city or region because that may be where God is concentrating

His attention. Therefore, these areas should demand your intercession focus. So allow the breath of God (the power of God according to the Illustrated Bible Dictionary) to blow upon you releasing the Lord's glorious presence that sets you free and guides you.

This is the month that the children of Israel exited Egypt. You may want to observe Nissan as a time that the Lord will deliver you from anything that separates you from Him. So whatever in you needs to be liberated, know that the Lord is the only One who can help you now and in the future! Deliverance needs to be in your quiver of weaponry especially during Nissan; deliverance is greatly enhanced this month because of the miracle of Israel's successful liberation.

Nissan exhibits the sign of a lamb. Lambs graze in a flock, faithfully following the shepherd. Being a follower is sometimes a mature choice, not a passive failure. The Jewish people made the choice to follow God, and not their own egos as people. In Egypt, as they vacillated between the twin forces of assimilation and oppression, they came to realize that relying on transient humans for their self-definition was national suicide, so they chose to follow the Lord. During this season make a cognitive decision to follow the Lord and allow the Holy Spirit to lead you in all things. Permit the Lord to deliver you from your own egocentricity (self-centeredness) and surrender your life to Him!

The Lord didn't free the children of Israel from Egypt without challenging them to make a commitment to Him so they could share in the redemptive process. The way that God challenged them, was by requiring each family to take a sheep, a symbol of Christ, and tie it to their bedpost for four days, and then sacrifice it on the altar of the Lord for Passover. Jesus, our sacrificial lamb, died once and for all and His Blood covers our sins for all times' sake. You must decide to tie the Lord to the bedposts of your heart and allow this to signify intimacy between you and Him.

During Nissan you should examine your relationship with the Lord and one another. More importantly do your relationships bring holiness, goodness, respect and clarity into the world? How often do you act out of your wounds and enslavement, creating more suffering rather than ease upon others? If during this season you feel as though you have brought more harm than good, then ask the Lord to forgive and deliver you of those things. Moreover, in what manner do you respond to the Bible's call to identify with the oppressed, with strangers, orphans, and widows on a daily basis? During Nissan you must ask yourself the question, "Do you participate in moving the world from hatred, racism and anger toward understanding, compassion and mutual respect?" You must also ask yourself whether you play a role in promoting enslavement, tyranny and hate in this world, or whether you're part of the solution!

The Lord has granted each human the freedom of choice, a free will, and in this way you're judged. The Bible's Exodus narrative describes that subsequent to each plague, Pharaoh was ready to relent and let the Jewish people go. But, each time God hardens Pharaoh's heart and he changes his mind. So one may ask, did Pharaoh have freedom of choice? If God hardened Pharaoh's heart, was he responsible for his action? Pharaoh indeed had freedom of choice. In fact, if God didn't "harden Pharaoh's heart" he would not have had freedom of choice at all. Who wouldn't let the Israelites go after witnessing just one of God's miracles? By hardening Pharaoh's heart, God actually leveled the playing field. With his heart hardened against the most natural and automatic response of letting the slaves go, Pharaoh was presented with a real palpable choice, his true self and true heart was able to emerge, and the answer was always, "NO!" During this season ask the Lord to assist you to make godly decisions and ask Him to align you properly with His will and purposes. Refuse, in the Spirit, to harden your hearts to God's destiny for your life and submit to His plans.

Passover is the festival this month and it means, "to pass." This is the day God passed over the houses of the sons of Israel because of the blood of the Lamb. Exodus 12 says, the blood will serve as a sign marking the houses where they lived and when I (the Lord) see the blood, I will pass over you. When I strike the land of Egypt, the death blow will not strike you. For the believer Jesus accomplished it all 2000 years ago on the 14th of Nissan! His Blood was shed and set upon the doorposts of your hearts! He officiated once for all and made Lappara (expiation) for our sins giving us access to the Kodesh Hakodashim (Holy of Holies), and His heart through the veil which was torn in His flesh gave us access into the very presence of the Lord! Jesus is the King of Judah, who will come back as the King of Kings and Lord of Lords! Please be reminded during the celebration of the Passover Feast that we are not observing something that has not affected us. We are celebrating that Jesus fulfilled every prophecy and consummated every Priestly and Kingly act that was set before Him, and He rules all of the kingdoms of the worlds earthly and heavenly. So during Passover allow the revelation of what Jesus did and who He is to saturate your being and receive that you are His people and He is your God!

It's during Nissan that you should ask that your mission in life be revealed. Honestly the Lord placed in you a passion to build a dwelling for Him to inhabit. Your godly purpose then, is to transform the earthly realm into an environment receptive to Divine truth and His Holy Presence, changing it into a place in which the goodness and perfection of God becomes the dominate reality in the earth today. Just like the children of Israel you and I must make a cognitive decision to operate, with freedom, in kingdom principles releasing hunger we have for earthly things. It's when you rest in the arms of the Lord that what you desire happens. During Nissan realize that relinquishing your ego and submitting to God's plans releases the peace you desperately seek.

It's the season to pray to God for your deliverance. Part of deliverance occurs as you watch what comes out of your mouth, because what you put into motion now with your speech may become a big problem for you in coming months. James 3:6 says it like this, *"The tongue also is a fire, a world of evil among the parts of the body. It corrupts the whole person, sets the whole course of his life on fire, and is itself set on fire by hell."* So partner with the Lord to place a watch on your tongue remembering that it's difficult to recall what your mouth has put into motion!

This is the month to put your right foot forward (be cognizant of what you're doing spiritually as well as naturally) and each believer should audit themselves to judge where they are spiritually. Be very watchful that you are led of the Holy Spirit. For your benefit ask for counsel during this time and if a decision isn't absolutely necessary to make, set it aside. I have learned that until the Lord opens a door of opportunity don't try to knock the door down. The best thing is to wait for God's proper timing.

The Hebraic word Nissan is known as the New Year of Kings, meaning there will be political shifts this month. It is the time kings go to war, so pray for proper decisions and prepare to go to war in the Spirit realm. During Nissan, pray intently for the president and other leaders to make godly decisions allowing the Lord to guide them in all they do.

Remember, when you have difficulty hearing the Lord, praise Him! When you need an answer for an issue, praise Him! When you're depressed and despondent, praise Him! Psalm 150 instructs us when we gather in our corporate services to, "Praise the Lord, *let everything that has breath, Praise the Lord*!"

The Gate of Praise
PROPHETIC DECLARATIONS

<u>*Declare prophetically over your life, church, and the seven spheres of influence that*</u>:

- The Gate of Praise is opened.
- The Lord with His brilliant light brings new life.
- Redemption is made available to all through the blood of Jesus.
- All are exalting Him for His mighty acts and deeds (Psalm 150)!
- Miracles will manifest through His presence.
- His breath has been released.
- Political shifts are benefiting the kingdom of God.
- The army of God is arising to do warfare against His enemies.
- Many are confessing the good things of God as they are delivered from their bondages now and in the future.
- Hearts are open to receive the presence of the Lord and His heavenly host.

"In order to transform our environment we <u>must</u> change."

Scripture References
Pslam 150

Prayer Proclamations

Psalm 18:3 *"Call to the Lord, who is worthy of praise, and I am saved from my enemies."*

Psalm 97:1-9 *"The Lord reigns, let the earth be glad ...*
Fire goes before him and consumes his foes on every side ...
The mountains melt like wax before the Lord ...
Zion hears and rejoices ...
For you, O Lord, are the Most High over all the earth."

Psalm 145:3 *"Great is the Lord and most worthy of praise; his greatness no one can fathom."*

****

PRAY THAT:
- We ask the Lord to transform our hearts
- We release a sound of extravagant praise that will arise as a weapon of war against our enemies
  (II Samuel 22:1; Psalm 18:3)
- Our praise confuses the enemy and his plans
  (II Chronicles 20)
- Praise demolishes all oppression and depression (Psalm 9:1-3)
- Our praise turns back our enemy (Zephaniah 3:14)
- We continually offer a sacrifice of praise as we confess the name of Jesus (Hebrews 13:15)
- Our praise changes the spiritual atmosphere (Isaiah 42:10-13)

REPENT and REFUSE TO PARTNER WITH:

- Apathy / Taking God's creative power for granted
- Lethargy / Rebellion - Refusal to use this weapon of spiritual warfare
- Religious, pious spirit and fear of man
- Doubt/Fear that God will not defeat our enemy
- Familiarity - Taking God's purpose for our lives for granted
- Ingratitude - Refusing to give Jesus the glory for our victories and blessings

****

Isaiah 12:6 *"Shout aloud and sing for joy, people of Zion, for great is the Holy One of Israel among you."*

Psalm 119:175 *"Let me live that I may praise you, and may your laws sustain me."*

Chapter Seven

The Gate of Revelation

"But when he, the Spirit of truth, comes, he will guide you into all truth. He will not speak on his own; he will speak only what he hears, and he will tell you what is yet to come."
~ *John 16:13*

Overview

According to Hebraic custom the <u>second month</u> (I King 6:1; the word Bul is a byword for Iyar) on the Jewish calendar is "<u>Iyar</u>" and it begins in April and ends in May on the Gregorian calendar. The tribe associated with this month is "<u>Issachar</u>," and it means "<u>reward</u> or <u>victory</u>." The gate name is "The Gate of <u>Revelation</u>."

General Information

The word "revelation" is God's communication to people concerning Himself, His moral standards, His purpose for His creation, and His plan of salvation, God is a personal Spirit distinct from the world; He is absolutely Holy and is invisible to the view of physical, finite, sinful minds. Other religions and philosophies result from the endless human quest for God; Christianity results from God's quest for lost mankind. As valuable as general revelation is for justice, honesty, and decency in the world today, it is not enough. The message of salvation was seen dimly through Old Testament sacrifices and ceremonies. It was seen more clearly as God redeemed the Israelites from enslavement in Egypt and as God disclosed to prophets the redemptive significance of His mighty acts of deliverance. However, even this fades away in the darkness to the revelation of the good news of God's mercy and His gracious gift of perfect righteousness seen through Jesus' death on the cross for our sins! This certainly is the greatest example of pure undefiled revelation!

Revelation of God is the content and process of the Lord making Himself known to people and all knowledge of the Lord comes by way of revelation. Human knowledge of God is revealed knowledge since God, and He alone, gives it. He bridges the gap between Himself and His creatures, disclosing Himself and His will to them, by God alone can the Lord be known!

Modern thought often questions the possibility and reality of revelation. Biblical faith affirms revelation is real because the personal Creator, God, has chosen to let human creatures know Him. The question remains, "How can a person know God?" The word "revelation" means an uncovering, a removal of the veil, and a disclosure of what was previously unknown. Revelation of God is the manifestation of Himself to mankind in such a way that men and women can know and fellowship with Him. Jesus explained to Peter, "Blessed are you, Simon son of Jonah, for this was not revealed to you by man, but my Father in heaven" (Matthew 16:17).

In summary, we can say that God has initiated the revelation of Himself to men and women. This revelation is understandable to humankind and makes it possible to know the Lord and grow in relationship with Him. His self endowed manifestation provides information about Himself for the purposes of leading men and women into His glorious presence.

Prophetically

Iyar signifies the month of radiance where the light of the Lord increases. If darkness tries to overtake you during this month say "No" by standing on the Bible, which needs to be deep within your heart. In particular you should read Isaiah chapter 60 to strengthen your spirit man, as you become a light for the Lord. Make no mistake, your Heavenly Father wants you walking in His light continually, however, this month you should focus all the more.

According to Jewish custom Iyar is the month of healing, therefore, "I Am" God your healer, manifests His Glory. Be careful not to murmur or complain during this time because negativity opens doors by which infirmities enter your life.

It's also important that you deal with your sinful nature (soul) by submitting wholeheartedly to the Lord. If you become passive to deal with your sin you may set a negative tone for the remainder of the year. Be very careful not to put ungodly things into motion, especially during Iyar.

Issachar is the scholarly tribe of Israel and the Sanhedren was mostly composed of this tribe. In particular, Issachar was the master of the "secret" of the Jewish calendar, they were:

"knower's who understood the times" (I Chronicles 12:32). His basic nature is contemplative and he serves as the "advisor" to his brethren in particular the king of Judah. Since the tribe associated with Iyar is Issachar you should be prepared to receive mysteries from the kingdom of God this month. In fact, align yourself to receive these revelations that are signs of your relationship with the Lord and be willing to receive godly counsel opening your ears to hear what the Lord is saying to you through others.

Furthermore, conscious (awareness) is the overlaying window for your soul and spirit. Permit the Lord to cleanse your conscious so the window that connects your spirit and soul are clean. Because your mind is the thinking process of your heart allow the Lord to fill your mind with His presence. If you have wrong information in your mind allow the Lord to correct it so that you will think properly. Since you and I should have the mind of Christ, this would be a good season to ask the Lord to impart His mind into yours!

Iyar is the month in which the Levites first raised the Tabernacle onto their shoulders to carry it through the desert and also when King Solomon laid the foundations for the Holy Temple onto the bedrock of Mount Moriah. Because significant events took place concerning the Temple of Israel expect the Lord to work within the Temple that exists in your heart. Allow the Lord to adjust you spiritually to bring you into proper alignment with His Kingdom.

Iyar is known by the name "Ziv" in the Hebrew Bible, a word which means "brightness" or "bud." It marks the passage from darkness to the brightness of revelation just as the children of Israel passed from the darkness of slavery to the brightness of freedom. When we, the children of God, walk with the Lord throughout our desert experiences and lift His expectations of who He says we are upon our shoulders, then He will dwell deep within our hearts guiding our steps. When you are determined to lay the foundations of His Holy Temple within the corridors of your hearts then your future, like the month of Iyar, will truly shine bright!

Once the sun begins to rise and a flower begins to bloom, there is no going back! A transformation has occurred! For this reason God told the Jews, who left Egypt, that if they obey the laws that He set forth, they will never suffer the diseases that He used as a weapon against the Egyptians. Moreover, He was saying to them that they, the Jews, would never again be Egyptian in any sense of the word. You need to come to a point where the Lord removes, entirely, Egypt (the things of this world) from the recesses of your heart. The Lord is saying that during this season you can have freedom in His Spirit if you align with Him and walk according to His concepts and precepts.

Manna, which nourished the Israelites throughout their forty year sojourn in the desert, began to fall during the fifteenth of Iyar. This provision forged awareness that God was involved in their (the Jews) material sustenance. Spiritually, revelation is much like manna; it's from our Heavenly Father and if we'll allow it His revelatory manna will sustain us. This was a necessary step to ready the Jews for the Torah even as it's a necessary step to prepare us to walk according to the Word of

God. We have to be conscious that the Lord is involved in our lives and realize that our deeds affect our fate. This awareness causes our latent love and trust in God to be actualized by our day-to-day reliance upon Him for our food and material goods. Physically, manna was perfect food for the Jews, as revelation is perfect food for you and I, manna caused no illnesses, leading the people to blossom just as God's revelation causes us no illness and we blossom!

The Israelites' entered the stage of world history with their war with Amalek, and this war took place during the month of Iyar (Exodus 17:8-16). The Amalekites victimized stragglers, the weak, tired and infirmed. In reality Amalek preyed upon the spiritual disarray of this newly escaped band of runaway slaves. So when Moses lifted his hands and directed the people's hearts toward heaven, even in the midst of battle, the children of Israel prevailed. Know that the Lord will prevail over your enemies, and He will give you the spiritual and natural strength to overcome. This is the month that supernatural spiritual strength will come upon you. So align yourself for the download and receive what the Lord has for you!

The fifteenth of Iyar is the second Passover. This was the day that Jews, who had been unable to bring their Passover offering to the Holy Temple by the first day of Passover, (either because they were too far away, or because they were ritually impure at the time), could bring their offerings and fulfill the commandments. This month literally signifies your second chance; it also indicates God's recognition that we are human and that our chief passion should be to serve Him. You have not lost out with the Lord; He is extending to you His heart of mercy and grace to walk in the anointing, purpose and destiny that He has given you. This is the season to come to a new level of faith and obey the Lord!

The Gate of Revelation
PROPHETIC DECLARATIONS

<u>*Declare prophetically over your life, church, and the seven spheres of influence that:*</u>

- The Gate of Revelation is opened.
- The glory of the Lord is seen in the church.
- The Body of Christ deals with their mind, will and emotions (soul) so that godly strength will occur.
- Godly revelation (secrets and mysteries from heaven) is released to the church.
- Minds are filled with thoughts of God.
- The Body of Christ watches intently what they allow inwardly and what they partner with outwardly.
- Godly counsel is sought.
- The conscience is cleansed so that the spirit and soul connect and are not cluttered with godless sinful thoughts.

"In order to transform our environment we <u>must</u> change."

Scripture References

Isaiah 60

Prayer Proclamations

<u>Ephesians 3:2</u> "Surely you have heard about the administration of God's grace that was given to me for you, that is, the mystery made known to me by revelation, as I have already written briefly. In reading this, then, you will be able to understand my insight into the mystery of Christ, which was not made known to men in other generations as it has now been revealed by the Spirit to God's holy apostles and prophets."

****

<u>PRAY THAT</u>:
- We ask the Lord to transform our hearts
- The light and glory of the Lord is increasing in our lives (Exodus 33:18)
- We experience God as our healer (Exodus 15:26)
- Our sinful nature (soul) is fully submitted to the Lord (Romans 8:4-9)
- We allow the Lord to fill our minds with His presence (Revelation 2:23)
- Our hearts are spiritually adjusted, and we are aligned with the kingdom (Colossians 3:1)
- The Lord will prevail over our enemies and give us spiritual and natural strength to overcome (Psalm 28:7)
- We are fully delivered out of darkness and into the brightness of freedom (I Peter 2:9)
- We position ourselves daily to receive fresh revelation from heaven (Galatians 1:12)

REPENT and REFUSE TO PARTNER WITH:

- Reasoning / Relying on our own thinking and strength
- Murmuring and Complaining
- Doubt and Unbelief
- Isolation / Pride / Self-focus
- Refusing to eradicate the enemy
- Negativity which opens the door to infirmity

****

II Chronicles 32:8 *"With him is only the arm of flesh, but with us is the Lord our God to help us and to fight our battles."*

I John 4:4 *"The one who is in you is greater than the one who is in the world."*

Chapter Eight

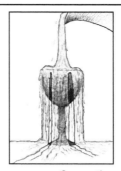

The Gate of Abundance

"And my God will meet all your needs according to His glorious riches in Christ Jesus."
~ Philippians 4:19

OVERVIEW

According to Hebraic custom the <u>third month</u> on the Jewish calendar is "<u>Sivan</u>" and it begins in May and ends in June on the Gregorian calendar. The tribe associated with this month is "<u>Zebulon</u>" and it is the month of "<u>giving</u> or <u>gifts</u>." The gate name is "The Gate of <u>Abundance</u>."

GENERAL INFORMATION

The word abundance as defined by the Webster's Encyclopedia of the Unabridged Dictionary is an extremely plentiful or over sufficient quantity or supply, it also means overflowing fullness or wealth. Abundance, from a biblical perspective is acknowledged to be a blessing from God; this can be seen from the witness of the Old Testament. God chose Abram and promised to bless him and make his name great

(Genesis 12:1-3). In the process, Abram became rich (Genesis 13:2). Further, we're told that God blessed Isaac, and he became very rich (Genesis 26:12-14). Solomon's wealth was seen as a sign of God's favor (I Kings 3:13, 10:23). Job, too, was blessed by God, and his wealth increased greatly (Job 42:12). These few examples do not allow us to assume that abundance rests only upon finances. In Psalm 36:7-8, King David declared, "How precious is your unfailing love! Both high and low among men find refuge in the shadow of your wings. They feast on the <u>abundance</u> of your house; you give them drink from your river of delights."

The Psalmist extends the imagery particularly to the godly (the believer). From the context it is preferable to limit the privilege of God's special protection to godly people. They alone have a right to find protection under the "Shadow of His wings." They alone have access to his "House," where the godly enjoy the communal meals as a token of God's goodness and provisions for them (Isaiah 65:13). They are given to drink, as it were, from the "River of Delights" and the "Fountain of Life."

The metaphors of food and drink denote the blessings of God for His people, both material and spiritual. Through Him the godly have food and drink as well as protection and the full enjoyment of their salvation. The word "Delights," in "River of Delights," evoke the illustration of the Garden of Eden, the experience of Eden, from which mankind was exiled, may be enjoyed by the godly in their fellowship with the Lord.

Therefore, abundance is not only equated to financial blessing, but also relates to the Lord and our relationship with

Him. As we seek refuge under the shadow of His loving arms, abundance will be revealed as never before.

Prophetically

Because the Jewish Bible (the Torah) was established during Sivan it's the month that we are to do spiritual business with the Lord. Allowing distractions to rule our lives or being out of spiritual alignment promotes delay. The story of Miriam in Numbers 12:1-16 exemplifies how delay and distractions stopped a nation. So be aware of "Miriam's" and be careful that you don't partner with those who might create distractions or who are not properly aligned with the Lord.

Miriam was greatly beloved by the Jewish people, however, when she touched Moses' anointing, God's vessel, she was stricken with leprosy and was exiled for seven days for cleansing. As a result Israel had to wait for her before they were able to go forth (Numbers 12:13-16). Whether they waited out of love or not, Miriam became a distraction creating a delay for the tribes of Israel. Therefore, be aware during Sivan, that there may be those whom you love and respect that may create confusion and delay. Be spiritually vigilant to recognize any postponements and then press through it! Moreover, this month it's important to stay in tune with the Lord being careful not to get ahead of Him because this too can create confusion and delays in your life.

Because this is the season to do spiritual business with the Lord remember bread cast on the water will return back to you the way you cast it (Ecclesiastes 11:1), so be attentive and careful what you sow, godly and ungodly. Ask the Lord to help you cast out blessings and not curses! Remember, it's better to give than it is to receive and during this time becoming a servant to the things of God will release favor over your life.

This month you will receive mercy for completion. The children of Israel were shown mercy when they were delivered from Egypt (pillar of fire, cloud by day, Red Sea parted, manna, shoes never wore out, etc). Look at it like this, you're half way to the finish line and you feel as though you're not going to make it. Then God refreshes you and you feel a sudden burst of energy to finish the race!

Sivan is also considered the wedding or covenant month because God made covenant with His people during this time. Make sure to enter into God's covenant forsaking satan's. This is the month that you decide to go God's way and not satan's. So be wise about your decisions (covenants) and follow God's lead then you'll succeed!

This month addresses time that you've wasted; therefore, you need to ask the Lord to forgive you for any wasted time. When the Lord restores, He restores faster than the wasted years brought the desolation. For example, if you wasted several years of your life living sinfully, what loss you experienced during that season will be restored quickly and in some cases instantaneously! So during Sivan shout, "Restore what the canker worms took and bring back one hundred fold what the enemy has stolen from me" (Joel 2:25 KJV).

It's during Sivan that the Lord desires for you to understand His principles of abundance. In reality you must allow the spiritual riches of His Kingdom to come, and then you must apply the principles of the kingdom in your life. Once God's Kingdom saturates you He and He alone will determine whether you'll receive earthly financial riches. You ought to be like Abraham; He sought the Lord with all his heart becoming His friend. As a result of this beautiful relationship, the bountiful blessings of the Lord were given to Abraham. He pursued the Lord with his whole heart and because of his deep abiding friendship with God, he was blessed; he didn't pursue the Lord to be blessed! Honestly, to give out of gratitude to the Lord is the highest form of giving. Being faithful with your tithe and offering does more for your spiritual maturity than you can possibly imagine. In essence, it releases the Holy Spirit to accomplish in your life His purposes for the kingdom. Therefore, when asked why you give tithe and offering your response should be "I'm glorifying the Lord!"

Why then does the Lord prosper the saints? He increases your yield so that by giving, you prove your yield is not your god! God doesn't prosper a person so they can move from a Ford to a Cadillac. The Lord blesses His people so that thousands of unsaved people can be reached with the Gospel and millions of believers can grow in kingdom maturity! So during this season of abundance give out of a heart of gratitude for what the Lord has done in your life and watch your harvest come with bountiful dividends.

During Sivan, it's important to review the previous months and recognize all the Lord has done in your life. So what you learned in Nissan and Iyar brings into Sivan a true understanding of God's blessings. So Sivan is a month to review the things the Lord has taught you and the time to evaluate how you've applied it.

In the Bible, the Harvest Festival coincides with the end of the barley harvest and is the beginning of the wheat harvest. Another name to consider during this time is (Hagha-Bikkurim) the Festival of the First Fruits, because on this day the first fruits of the wheat harvest were brought to the Temple in Jerusalem. The Mishnah (a paragraph that forms the basic part of the Jewish Talmud) gives vivid descriptions of how the first fruits were brought to the Temple on this festival, to the accompaniment of singing and dancing, the playing of instruments and the beating of drums. This shows a much different perspective of how our tithe and offering services are held. During Sivan, you should bring your tithe, offerings and first fruit offerings to the storehouse with a heart of great celebration! You must be careful to give with a joyful heart because giving without joy opens the door for satan to snare you. In your giving do so as the Lord directs so you will receive His blessing.

Since Sivan is the month the children of Israel received their Torah this would be a good time to allow the Lord to help you set boundaries around your life. In reality people don't know how to set a boundary by saying "no" so during this time the Lord will help you to say "no" to things that are not good for you spiritually. He will also assist you to understand how to have proper relationships without being dependent emotionally on others!

According to Jewish custom Sivan is the month of the twins, in particular Jacob and Esau. When Jacob stole the birthright from his brother it signified that he was passionate about going the way of the Lord, Esau on the other hand was not so passionate! During this time allow the Lord to deposit within your heart a passion to serve Him at greater levels because this is the month to choose which direction you need to go spiritually, God's way or satan's. Be careful that you don't pursue anything that is not important to the kingdom, because your wrong decisions now will surely plague you in month's to come!

Because the festival of Pentecost (Shavuot) triggered several miraculous events, like the day of Pentecost in Acts chapter two, you should decide whether or not you want to be a catalyst for the Lord. To be a catalyst means to "trigger an event." During this time, initiate something for the Lord that occurs from right alignment and obedience. So this is the time for methodical progression and seeking godly counsel for your future.

Unlike the children of Israel you should be aware of tributaries and be careful to stay on the main river flow of the Lord. Tributaries create a delay and postponement causing a setting aside of the plans of the Lord. So be careful to stay within the main banks of your river flow. This is the month of the left foot, meaning you should connect your walk with your speech. Remember out of your mouth your heart speaks so be sure your heart is in the right place so when you speak you'll be delivering God's message and not your own. It's the time to be who you are in God's Kingdom not someone else; you cannot operate in the realm of religiosity or status-quo during Sivan because what you decree sets your spiritual tone for the future. In other words, what you speak now is what you'll walk at the end of this month.

Look, during Sivan, to complete things quicker than ever before. It was during this time that Nehemiah rebuilt the walls and gates of Jerusalem, in 52 days while it took seventy years for the destruction to occur. So what the enemy has meant for evil to cause you to labor for long periods of time the Lord is increasing the anointing for quick completion!

Therefore abundance may be monetary or it could be health or spiritual blessing. Can anyone categorize any of these three blessings as less than one another? When the Lord blesses He does so thoroughly and each of us must be filled with gratitude for His blessings no matter how they manifest. Just because the Lord may not be blessing us financially doesn't mean we're not blessed. We ought to take a careful inventory of how the Lord is blessing us and then rejoice for His eternal kindness!

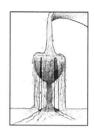

The Gate of Abundance
PROPHETIC DECLARATIONS

<u>*Declare prophetically over your life, church, and the seven spheres of influence that*</u>:

- The Gate of Abundance is opened.
- God's principles for abundance are understood (Matthew 6:1-4, 33).
- Joyful and generous gifts of special offerings are given above first fruit and tithe.
- Alignment with the Lord and those He has chosen to represent Him (apostles, prophets, pastors, teachers and evangelists) will occur.
- Compassion (mercy) is shown to one another.
- Mercy is experienced as God's directives are accomplished.
- A covenant is made with God choosing His path not the wrong path.
- Caution is used through careful speech to prevent a double standard with my actions.
- Wasted time, effort, and wealth are restored.

"In order to transform our environment we <u>must</u> change."

Scripture References

Numbers 12:1-16   Proverbs 10:9
Ecclesiastes 11:1   Joel 2:25

Prayer Proclamations

I Timothy 6:17-19 "Command those who are rich in this present world not to be arrogant nor to put their hope in wealth, which is so uncertain, but to put their hope in God, who richly provides us with everything for our enjoyment. Command them to do good, to be rich in good deeds, and to be generous and willing to share. In this way they will lay up treasure for themselves as a firm foundation for the coming age, so that they may take hold of the life that is truly life."

****

PRAY THAT:
- We ask the Lord to transform our hearts
- We always seek first the heavenly treasures (Matthew 6:19; Philippians 3:8; Proverbs 23:23)
- God gives us understanding of His principles of abundance (Matthew 6:33)
- We have a heart for joyful giving (II Corinthians 8:1-9)
- We are good stewards of God's blessings (I Corinthians 4:1-2)
- Our speech is connected to our walk (Proverbs 10:9)
- We stand against the idolatry of materialism (Colossians 3:5)

REPENT and REFUSE TO PARTNER WITH:
- Idolatry – Treasure on earth / Mammon / Worldly Power
- Anti-Christ – Anything that refuses to bow to Jesus
- Familiarity with the great gift of salvation
- Lack of faith for physical and emotional provision
- Accusation against our brothers, gossip, lies
- Compulsive or manipulative giving that expects something in return

****

Proverbs 8:18 *"With me are riches and honor, enduring wealth and prosperity."*

Ephesians 1:18 *"I pray also that the eyes of your heart may be enlightened in order that you may know the hope to which he has called you, the riches of his glorious inheritance in the saints."*

Chapter Nine

The Gate of Righteousness

"Sow for yourselves righteousness, reap the fruit of unfailing love, and break up your unplowed ground; for it is time to seek the Lord, until he comes and showers righteousness on you."
~ Hosea 10:12

OVERVIEW

According to Hebraic custom the <u>fourth month</u> (Jeremiah 39; Zechariah 8:19) on the Jewish calendar is "<u>Tammuz</u>." It begins in June and ends in July on the Gregorian calendar. The tribe associated with Tammuz is "<u>Rueben</u>" and it means "<u>wondrous recognition</u>." The gate is "The Gate of <u>Righteousness</u>."

GENERAL INFORMATION

To be righteous means to live a holy and upright life, in accordance to God's standard. The word "righteousness" comes from a root word that means "straightness." It refers to a state that conforms to an authoritative standard; therefore, righteousness refers to a moral concept. In reality God's character is the definition and source of all righteousness (Genesis 18:25; Deuteronomy 32:4; Romans 9:14). Moreover, the righteousness of man is defined in terms of God's.

In the Old Testament the term "righteous" is used to define our relationship with God (Psalm 50:6) and with other people (Jeremiah 9:24). In the context of relationship, righteous (moral) action promotes the peace and well being of humans in their relationship to one another. For example, Adam and Eve would have acted righteously in their relationship with God if they had obeyed Him, because His commands defined that relationship. The Ten Commandments and laws defined Israel's relationship with God. To obey those laws was to act righteously, because such obedience maintained the covenant relationship between God and His people.

The sacrificial system in the Old Testament and the cross of Jesus in the New Testament show people's need for righteousness. Sin is disobedience to the terms that define our relationship with God and with other people. Since the fall of man in the Garden of Eden, people have been inherently unrighteous.

As the prophet Isaiah said, "We are all like an unclean thing, and all our righteousness's are like filthy rags; we all fade as leaf, and our iniquities, like the wind, have taken us away" (Isaiah 64:6). We cannot be righteous in the sight of God on our own merits. Therefore, people must have God's righteousness imparted or transferred to them.

The cross of Jesus is a public demonstration of God's righteousness. God accounts or transfers the righteousness of Christ to those who trust in Him (Romans 4:3-22; Galatians 3:6; Philippians 3:9). We do not become righteous because of our inherent goodness; God sees us as righteous because of our identification by faith with His Son Jesus Christ. So as we enter into this month of Righteousness we need to recognize that our moral uprightness doesn't happen because of what we do but rather because of what Jesus did!

PROPHETICALLY

It's the time when Aaron fashioned the Golden Calf and blamed the Israelites without taking responsibility for his own actions (Exodus 30:20-22). Therefore, this reminds us that when our actions are ungodly and we feel frightened or angry, and blame others we must repent and ask the Lord to forgive us. Therefore, Tammuz is a time to reflect on overcoming, with the help of the Lord, your worst impulses and bondages.

Because the children of Israel worshipped the Golden Calf this month it's the time to do the opposite by being brilliant through worship of the Lord (extravagant respect or devotion). When the Jews worshipped the Golden Calf and Moses broke the Ten Commandments it was a result of idolatry. So during Tammuz ask the Lord to deliver you of any thing that would cause you to be idolatrous or inconsistent in keeping covenants with Him or one another.

Tammuz is the time to speak out who you are in God's Kingdom. If you're not aware of who you are then you may be speaking negatively about who God says you are in Him.

Therefore, this is the month to ask the Lord to reveal your <u>spiritual identity</u>. Every time you speak or think wrongly about yourself, you're saying to the Lord that you disagree with what He's created (this applies to you spiritually not to the natural identity you have adopted along the way). You must remember that you're divinely and uniquely made in His image and repent for believing otherwise.

The month of Tammuz falls in the heat of the summer when grass dries up and flowers begin to fall. In the Middle East, this is the burning season when no rain falls and at midday the heat is too intense to work. Even so when things feel dry spiritually this is a good time to soberly seek the Holy Spirit about the condition of your heart. Also it's a time to be sensitive to what the Lord is doing in the earth and pray intently for His will to be performed.

Jewish legend says that this was the month that Adam and Eve were driven out of Eden to wander in the harsh world and labor to get bread out of the earth. It's also the time when Moses struck the rock in anger, trying to get water from it. So this is the time to repent for any activity that causes you to go your way rather than God's. Moreover, this is the month of return because when Moses struck the rock the water burst forth and the well of healing and life came forth. So remember what the enemy has meant for evil the Lord will return it for good.

By revelation, the first of Tammuz is the anniversary of the birth of Joseph, the son of Jacob. Throughout the problematic seasons of Joseph's life he raises, every time, to a greater level. In the end he rules over all Egypt and saves his family from the famine. Even so, the things that you are going through, the feelings of despair and anger will be uprooted this month if you'll align with the Lord and allow Him to deliver you.

This is the month of the letter "Chet," meaning light radiating from your eyes. One of satan's purposes is to put out the spiritual lamp that burns in your heart. So during Tammuz you must allow the inner radiance of the Lord to counter satan's attacks. Therefore, what the Lord has deposited in you over the previous months needs to be released now so you can counter the enemy's attacks. Begin to think properly about who you are in God's Kingdom and allow His light to eliminate the darkness that tries to encroach upon you, in Jesus Name!

This is the visual film strip month that enables you to watch your life adjust and progress. Issues that keep coming up during this time may be things that the Lord wants to heal. It's during this period that you need to realize that doing the same thing over and over expecting different results is "insanity." Allow the Lord to break anything that is habitual and counterproductive in your life.

This is the month of the crab so during this time remove the hard outer shell (bondages that separate you from God) that restricts your relationship with the Lord, so that you can enter the next month with victory. If you're not willing to surrender your life to the Lord you will not be triumphant in the month of Av (the next Jewish month).

You must ask God to place a guard around your heart and eyes because satan is out to deceive you, so it's a time when you can easily be thrown off guard. It's a month for fasting and praying and these two weapons of war will prove to be vitally important to guard your eyes and heart from the works of the evil one.

The word Tammuz reads in Hebrew; "tam" meaning connect together or consummate. Be careful who you enter into covenant with, because the results of unwise decisions will be exposed in later months. A haphazard agreement must not occur during Tammuz. Be careful to watch who's around you and seek counsel so that you will not be caught unaware. Be cautious about business partnerships and pray over every covenant.

During Tammuz several events occurred that were critical in Jewish history. For instance, Joshua's prayer stopped the sun, Ezekiel's vision of the chariots occurred, in 586 B.C. Jerusalem's walls were breached and the Temple services were disrupted, in 70 A.D. Jerusalem's walls were breached again and in 1976 the Entebbe rescue took place. Also, Tammuz 17 was the name of the Iraqi nuclear reactor destroyed by Israel in 1981. It was so named because the 17th of Tammuz is the day that Jerusalem was sieged prior to the destruction of the Temple by Nebuchadnezzar, and Saddam Hussein was known to fancy himself as the heir to Nebuchadnezzar's fallen dynasty. Does this mean that the month of Tammuz is "a bad month?" Far from it, it's the month of challenge and confrontation. Without challenge, there's no growth, without confrontation, there's no way to see things the way they are. So what should you look for during this month? The attacks of the enemy are elevated during Tammuz and you should take a serious stand against him! Be vigilant to watch and walk in high realms of discernment. Allow your challenges to spiritually mature you and the confrontations to expose where you are and also where you're going spiritually!

During Tammuz it's important to know that when your mental imagery is in tune with the Lord's vision of reality, it can move you toward divine inspiration. This can only happen when you're not blocking out the Lord's truth with your agendas (which are so subtle that many times we're not always aware of their existence). When your filters are on, it creates inner chaos and your fears promote fantasies of dread. During this month trust the Lord and not those wrong emotions. Permit the Lord to lead you and fix your heart on His!

The Gate of Righteousness
PROPHETIC DECLARATIONS

<u>Declare prophetically over your life, church, and the seven spheres of influence that</u>:

- The Gate of Righteousness is opened.
- Recognition of the Lord who cleanses all hearts causing righteousness to arise!
- All worship (extravagant respect or devotion) the Lord rather than idols.
- The Lord has wonderfully made all things.
- The light of the Holy Spirit is radiating from His church transforming the city.
- All are discovering who we are in God's Kingdom.
- The hard outer shell formed by isolation and independence is broken and all will walk in victory.
- Hearts and eyes are focused upon the Lord so they are not thrown off by the enemy.
- All will carefully choose with whom they enter into covenant.

"In order to transform our environment we <u>must</u> change."

Scripture References

Genesis 18:25
Deuteronomy 32:4
Jeremiah 9:24-25
Isaiah 64:6
Psalm 50:6
Romans 4:3-22
Romans 9:14
Galatians 3:6
Philippians 3:9

Prayer Proclamations

<u>*Genesis 15:6*</u> *"Abram believed the Lord, and he credited it to him as righteousness."*

<u>*I Samuel 15:22*</u> *"Does the Lord delight in burnt offerings and sacrifices as much as in obeying the voice of the Lord. To obey is better than sacrifice and to heed is better than the fat of rams."*

****

<u>PRAY THAT</u>:
- We ask the Lord to transform our hearts
- As we walk in faith our prayers <u>are</u> being answered (Isaiah 26:3, 65:24; I Kings 8:56)
- We are righteous through trusting in Jesus (Isaiah 50:10; Psalm 34:22)
- The Lord will reveal to us our spiritual identity (Genesis 28:15; Acts 9:1-22)
- God reveals how we must shift to participate with Him in becoming righteous (Ezekiel 33:19; Luke 10:27-28; Galatians 6:8)
- Idolatry, the spirit of Baal, and the anti-Christ spirit be destroyed (I John 2:18-27)

<u>REPENT and REFUSE TO PARTNER WITH</u>:
- Thinking we don't need cleansing – Pride
- Doubt that God is answering us
- Shame or Self-pity that would keep us focused on our sin

- Disbelief that Jesus' Blood can purify us or our family
- Refusal to change or give up our sin as God reveals it to us
- Making anything more important than Jesus and the church
- Passivity and lack of accountability for what God has destined us to accomplish for Him

****

<u>Proverbs 12:28</u> "In the way of righteousness there is life; along that path is immortality."

<u>Isaiah 61:10</u> "I delight greatly in the Lord; my soul rejoices in my God. For he has clothed me with garments of salvation and arrayed me in a robe of righteousness, as a bridegroom adorns his head like a priest, and as a bride adorns herself with her jewels."

Chapter Ten

The Gate of Wisdom

"But the wisdom that comes from heaven is first of all pure, then peace-loving, considerate, submissive, full of mercy and good fruit, impartial and sincere."
~ James 3:17

OVERVIEW

According to Hebraic custom the <u>fifth month</u> (Numbers 33: 38; Zechariah 7:3) on the Jewish calendar is "<u>Av</u>" and it begins in July and ends in August on the Gregorian calendar. The tribe associated with this month is "<u>Simeon</u>," and it means "<u>To hear or be concerned</u>." From biblical and historical information about the tribes the gate name is "The Gate of <u>Wisdom</u>."

GENERAL INFORMATION

Wisdom is the ability to judge correctly and to follow the best course of action, based on knowledge and understanding. Proverbs 9:10 gives us an understanding of wisdom, "The

81

fear of the Lord is the beginning of wisdom, and knowledge of the Holy One is understanding." J.I. Packer put it this way, "Wisdom is, in fact, the practical side of moral goodness," and Bill Gothard said that, "Wisdom is seeing life from God's point of view."

The Apostle Paul declared that the message of the cross is foolishness to the Greeks and a stumbling block to the Jews. But to those who believe, said Paul, this "foolishness of God" is the "Wisdom of God" (I Corinthians 1:18-25). While this message is desired by all, few end up following its reasoning, against the wisdom of God, Paul contrasted (being noticeably different from something), "the wisdom of this world" (I Corinthians 1:20, 3:19), "human wisdom" (I Corinthians 2:4), "the wisdom of men" (I Corinthians 2:6), "the wisdom of this age" (I Corinthians 2:6), and "man's wisdom" (I Corinthians 2:13). The biblical concept of wisdom on the other hand, is quite different from the worldview. Through the filter of worldly wisdom, philosophy and human rational the mysteries of existence and knowledge of the universe are determined. The biblical principle of wisdom is that people should humble themselves before God in reverent worship, obedient to His commands, fearing His awe-inspiring ways. Therefore, the Gate of Wisdom isn't defined by the wisdom of man or this world; nor is it a societal gate meant to open pathways to social acceptance or worldly success. Its wisdom based upon God who generously gives to all who ask (James 1:5). As you gain heavenly insight into your earthly issues you're able to understand the complexities of life with supernatural understanding. Therefore, the riches found in God's wisdom bring great peace to a tumultuous situation. It unlocks unmerited favor that cannot be interpreted from our natural mindedness but only understood through God's heavenly kingdom!

There are three ways in which a person can define wisdom. <u>First</u>, wisdom is considered by many to be simply the art of learning how to succeed in life. Apparently, ancient people learned very early that there was orderliness to the world in which they lived. They also learned that success and happiness came from living in accordance with that orderliness (Proverbs 22:17 – 24:22). <u>Second</u>, wisdom is considered by some to be a philosophical study of the essence of life. Certainly, much of the Books of Job and Ecclesiastes seem to deal with just such existential issues of life (Job 30:29-31). <u>Third</u>, the real essence of wisdom is spiritual, for life is more than just living by a set of rules and being rewarded in some physical manner. Undoubtedly, this sense of wisdom comes from God (Proverbs 2:6). Thus, though it will involve observation and instruction, wisdom really begins with God and one's faith in Him as Lord and Savior (Proverbs 1:7; Job 28:28). Heavenly inspired wisdom occurs when you surrender to the Holy Spirit allowing Him to guide you. It does not rest upon a person because of their intelligence, education or capability. It occurs as you yield to humility and recognize that God's plans are more important than yours.

Prophetically

Av is the month to be humble because humility ushers in wealth, honor and life (Proverbs 22:4). You must stay encouraged in the Lord listening intently to His voice for guidance, seeking His assistance along the way. Because many catastrophic events occurred to Israel historically during Av, be alert to the strategies of the enemy. Remember, just because you've had a bad day doesn't mean that satan will back off from attacking you, in reality, he's probably behind your bad day! Honestly, satan and his minions will attack even more if you allow them to know that you're not doing well. So not only are you to be aware of satan's tactics every day, you especially need to be more watchful this month, watchful of the enemy's attacks and vigilant about how you communicate those attacks. That's why, during Av, the Lord deals with your complacency to war against the tactics of the enemy even more so than other months. The best way to walk a victorious life is to stay <u>proactive</u> in your obedience to the Lord. If you stay at a high level of spiritual intensity, this is the month that He will bless you, if not; the Lord will challenge you to change.

This is the month of "Tet" and it resembles the womb, during this month things will be birthed, so be very careful what you create during Av. Many of you are in trouble because you continue to think that your way is the best way. You'll need to be proactive to interact with the Lord and His delegated authority listening intently to their counsel. The results of this month will be glaringly clear about the path you chose to take, if you listen to counsel you'll succeed, if you listen to yourself you won't! Also the Lord records what we do in a book, meaning He chronicles our actions (Revelation 20:11-12), so be watchful of your activity because it is very important.

To "hear" in Hebrew means to understand or receive. Regarding hearing and receiving, this is a prophetic month (Amos 3:8, "The lion has roared – who will not fear? The Sovereign Lord has spoken – who can but prophesy?") to listen keenly to the Lord and put into motion those things that He has spoken to you. The twelve spies, led by Joshua and Caleb, were sent by Moses to the land of Canaan in Tammuz and reported their findings to him and the children of Israel in the month of Av (Numbers 13:1-25). Ten spies spoke evil of the land that God had promised Israel (Numbers 13:26-33) and the people accepted (heard – received) the evil tongue (Numbers 14:1-45). Thus the thread that is woven throughout Av is the adjustment of your spiritual hearing and when you heed what the Lord says about an issue it results in acting wisely, if not you're speaking wrongly about what God calls blessed and you're operating unwisely. If God speaks to you and you decide not to listen, you will be held accountable for your decision. As a matter of fact, it's during Av that the Lord will judge what you've put in motion over the past several months, that's why it's important to stay proactive (a step toward wisdom) with the Lord. When you partner with Him to cast off things that are ungodly, He will deliver you of them. So when you acknowledge and walk in obedience to the Lord you become people of wisdom.

The Lord's will is constantly executed throughout life and into eternity. However, this month the Divine will of the Father is implemented at an increased level. Just as the Lord examined the Temple in Jerusalem and allowed its destruction in 70 A.D., He's inspecting what's firmly built in your life and what is not. He may look at what you've established and determine that it's best to tear it down rather than repair it or He may destroy it in order to reconstruct it. So don't be disappointed if what you thought was godly or felt was formed on a firm foundation crumbles to the ground.

Because of the amount of destruction that has occurred throughout history during Av, be particularly sensitive to how the Lord is moving upon the earth, meaning you probably should be alert to the earth's contractions. Many earthquakes, natural disasters and trauma may occur in Av, so earnestly pray for protection and insight as to what the Lord is doing through these events. It could be that either judgment has been released because of disobedience or breakthrough occurs because of obedience. So ask God for revelation about what He's doing and pray for wisdom to spiritually transact this month.

On the ninth and tenth of the month of Av in the year 70 A.D., the Roman legions in Jerusalem smashed through the fortress tower of Antonia into the Holy Temple and set it afire, in the blackened remains of the sanctuary lay more than the ruins of the great Jewish revolt for their political independence. To many Jews, it appeared that Judaism itself had been shattered beyond repair and hopelessness and despair flooded many of them. During this month be careful to not allow hopelessness or despair (witchcraft) to overwhelm you. If circumstances are overpowering then allow the wisdom of the Lord to help you prevail! Lean heavily upon the Holy Spirit during Av and watch His Glory smash those issues that have become troublesome to you.

This is the month where God's Kingdom advances through your partnership, so be aware of your alignments and alliances. You must walk in keen discernment peering into the Spirit realm to recognize the strategies that the enemy uses through opposing counsel and ungodly advice. Be alert to accusations that will tear you down. Also refute accusations that are coming against those whom God has placed over you. That's why, during Av, the Lord deals with your complacency to war against the tactics of the enemy even more so than other months. The best way to walk a victorious life is to stay <u>proactive</u> doing everything the Lord has asked. If you stay at a high level of spiritual intensity, this is the month that He will bless you, if not your Heavenly Father will provoke you to change.

Have you ever been in a relationship that ended? Or watched a great chance come and go? Have you ever made a choice you later wished you could reverse? How many times in your life have you said "I should have" or "if only…" It's difficult enough to let go of something you have in hand. Often a large part of the pain comes from the sense of loss over what you could have had. Displeasure with your circumstances and sadness for squandering your potential can cause you to function in an ungodly manner. It's extremely difficult to progress when you're continually looking at issues that are negative in your life. If in your frustration about what you've lost, you begin to focus on what's right rather than what's wrong, a solution will arise from the ashes. So during this month first repent for any activity that may have caused the Lord to set something in motion because of disobedience. Then hear what He's saying about your situation and trust Him to show you.

The Gate of Wisdom
PROPHETIC DECLARATIONS

Declare prophetically over your life, church, and the seven spheres of influence that:

- The Gate of Wisdom is opened.
- Any sinful activity is confessed.
- A greater level of spiritual intensity is experienced.
- The Holy Spirit is guiding me to make proper spiritual shifts.
- The divine will of the Father be executed.
- A spiritual birthing to occur.
- Mercy for any ungodly choices made in the past.
- The prophetic voice that unlocks the kingdom of God will be heard.
- The Lord tears down and rebuilds whatever is not built upon His foundation.
- Natural disasters do not occur and divine protection is released.
- Acceptance of Christ and holiness fills lives.
- Godly wisdom to partner and align spiritually occurs so that the kingdom of God will advance.
- Revelation of spiritual warfare is released to counter the tactics of the enemy.

"In order to transform our environment we <u>must</u> change."

Scripture References

Proverbs 22:4
Revelations 20:11-12

PRAYER PROCLAMATIONS

Proverbs 1:5 *"Let the wise <u>listen</u> and add to their learning and let the discerning get guidance."*

Proverbs 8:34-35 *"Blessed is the man who <u>listens</u> to me, watching daily at my doors, waiting at my doorway. For whoever finds me finds life and receives favor from the Lord."*

****

PRAY THAT:
- We ask the Lord to transform our hearts
- We are walking in humility to receive guidance (Proverbs 1:5; James 1:5-6)
- We are willing to seek guidance from spiritual authority (Proverbs 15:31, 18:15, 25:12)
- We are willing to apply what we learn/receive (Matthew 13:23)
- We are willing to wait on God's timing (Proverbs 8:34-35; Luke 8:15)
- We have attentiveness and intensity to seek and hear God's voice (Proverbs 2:1-5; Luke 10:38-42)
- We refuse to partner with accusation, gossip or ungodly counsel (Romans 1:29-2:11)
- We have true love of wisdom (Proverbs 4:7-9, 8:1-36)

REPENT and REFUSE TO PARTNER WITH:
- Arrogance/religious spirit that refuses to admit limited understanding
- Rebellion/conceit that refuses to seek counsel
- Laziness/selfishness that will not apply revelation for the good of the kingdom

- Impatience/ Control/ Manipulation
- Choosing worldly wisdom over God's counsel
- Gossip, slander, backbiting, judgmental spirit
- Partnership with the world

****

<u>Ecclesiastes 5:1</u> *"Guard your steps when you go to the house of God. <u>Go near to listen</u> rather than to offer the sacrifice of fools, who do not know that they do wrong."*

<u>James 1:19</u> *"Everyone should be <u>quick to listen</u>, slow to speak, and slow to become angry."*

Chapter Eleven

The Gate of Repentance

*"If my people, who are called by my name, will humble themselves
and pray and seek my face and turn from their wicked ways
then will I hear from heaven and will forgive their sin
and will heal their land."*
~ II Chronicles 7:14

OVERVIEW

According to Hebraic custom the sixth month (Nehemiah 6:15) on the Jewish calendar is "Elul" and it begins in August and ends in September on the Gregorian calendar. The tribe associated with this month is "Gad." This tribe was comprised of warriors fit for battle. They were men who could handle shield, sword, spear and bow. The Gadites were considered fierce fighters whose faces were like that of lions; their seed (legacy) was prepared for continuous battle against the enemies of Israel, as the blessing goes, "They came with the heads of people." The gate name is "The Gate of Repentance."

General Information

It is believed that the prophet Gad, who was King David's personal seer and counselor (II Samuel 24:11-17), came from the tribe of Gad. The Lord spoke powerfully through this prophet, and he was great in the nation of Israel. Since the tribe of Gad produced prophets, they were not only powerful fighting men in the natural; they were also mighty warriors in the Spirit. They fought not only for their country but contended for righteousness as well, which is precisely what we are called to do! This month permit the Lord to infuse you with a warrior spirit poised to fight for righteousness!

Moreover, the month of Elul signifies that it is the time to prepare for the coming Jewish New Year and the Ten Days of Awe from Rosh Hashanah to Yom Kippur. From a biblical perspective preparation during this month involves repentance.

The word repentance means, a turning away from sin, disobedience, or rebellion and a turning back to God (Matthew 9:13; Luke 5:32). In a more general sense, it means a change of mind (Genesis 6:6-7) or a feeling of remorse or regret for past conduct (Matthew 27:3). From a natural mindset, the word repentance carries with it shame or embarrassment. However, examining the act of repentance you will find life and mercy. For it's through repentance, the act of turning from sin, that the Lord forgives drawing you closer to His heart.

Therefore, instead of repentance being negative, it opens the way for a closer relationship with Him, becoming one of the most positive assets of our Christian experience. So please see repentance as a positive rather than a negative act and place it in your quiver of spiritual weapons! Remember repentance can only operate to its fullest extent when you allow the Holy Spirit to convict you of any disobedience. Ask the Lord to convict (find guilty) you of any trespasses that you may have committed. This process will cause a sensitivity to arise in your heart that creates a bulwark (strong support or protection) against anything that could separate you from Him! Always remember repentance brings God's mercy and forgiveness that ushers in His presence and His presence is what we humbly desire!

Prophetically

During this month you should be aware that the Lord is examining your life to see where you have held Him in contempt (disrespect). It is your responsibility to discover, in partnership with God, any sinful behavior in your life and repent for that activity; remembering that as you walk in a spirit of <u>contrition</u> and <u>holiness</u> you are defeating satan! As Christians it's important to repent daily for any sin, but it is particularly significant during Elul. Historically, this is the month of personal introspection (examination of one's own thought or feelings) as well as remembering and repenting for ones transgressions.

The month of Elul is considered a season of divine grace. It was during this time that Moses received the second tablets (the Ten Commandments – Exodus 32, 34:27-28), reassuring the children of Israel that the Lord had forgiven them for worshipping the Golden Calf. So it is with us, allow the Holy Spirit to direct you to repent for anything you have done covertly (secret) or overtly (open).

It is paramount that you are in right alignment with the Lord.

This is the month to find your place in the camps or ministries of the Lord. Many people miss their window of opportunity to find their spiritual place because of mistrust. If you have an area of mistrust it will close the window of possibilities with the Lord, as a result, when an occasion presents itself to connect with God's window, if you haven't dealt with mistrust, you may not want to partner with it. The outcome is that you may isolate trying to create a place (ministry) that feels good to you when in fact it isn't right with God (deception). In all actualities mistrust is a root of rejection that stops your crossing over into what God wants for your life. If you're not careful, you'll find yourself in your wilderness alone, which no one needs, <u>so connect</u>!

There is more to Elul than preparation alone; it's also a time of <u>giving</u> and <u>prayer</u>. In ancient times Elul was the "New Year for Tithes" and it remains today the time when annual pledges regarding charitable gifts should be <u>reviewed</u> and <u>renewed</u>. During this season you may consider supporting, to a greater degree, the church (storehouse) where the Lord has planted you, because it's a time, as you follow God's lead, blessings and good fortune will overtake you. This is the month to pray like you've never prayed before. So pray continually asking the Lord for divine assistance and insight, don't let the enemy steal your time, take it back in the name of Jesus! Elul is considered an auspicious (suggesting that there is a good chance of success) time to enter into covenants and weddings. Actually the word "Elul" in Jewish terminology is an acronym of Song of Songs 6:3, "I am my beloveds and my beloved is mine," where the Beloved is God and the "I" is God's people. In Aramaic, the word "Elul" means, "search," which is appropriate, because this is a time of year when you search your heart. It's during the month of

Elul that you are reminded to recapture your relationship with the Lord. So you should re-examine your lives to make amends with your loving Heavenly Father!

During Elul it's a custom to blow the shofar to wake-up those who are spiritually asleep. It's meant to rouse us from <u>complacency</u>. Elul is a time to ask forgiveness for the wrongs that we have done to others. Mark 11:25 says, "And when you stand praying, if you hold anything against anyone, forgive him, so that your Father in heaven may forgive you your sins." Be careful to watch your attitude and don't allow the enemy to destroy the relationship the Lord is building with those He has placed over and around you. If you do not heed this prophetic declaration, you may pay a price later in the year.

It's important to know that during this month rewards will manifest because of what you've done in the Spirit realm. This is a time to be rewarded for allowing the Holy Spirit to lead you throughout the previous months. However, if you're not careful, you'll carry a burden longer than what is required and it will <u>deplete</u> you. There must be a time when you receive a reward, thus laying down the burden. You must learn how to be a proper burden bearer recognizing them and asking the Lord for strength to walk them out not allowing agony to take its place (Matthew 11:28-30). Apostle Chuck Pierce says "Burden usually has seven days of agony and then a one year process in order to transition into God's plan for your life." The key to remember is that you must be a burden bearer but you must transition out of agony quickly. When we can't stand under the burden the Lord says, "Bring it under me."

Elul is the month where "The King is in the field, so approach Him and allow His countenance to shine upon you." Many are fearful to approach the Lord because they have an improper comprehension of Him. To receive from the Lord you must see Him as your loving Heavenly Father. While it's important to have relationship continually, this month is particularly significant so approach Him with a contrite heart and receive the benefits of relationship. You must learn a dimension of awe where you can experience the wonder of God allowing Him to pour into you; it's a place of great joy.

Elul is also the month of "YUD" – meaning appointed mercy from the hand of God and you need to grab that mercy with passion. Just because you missed something doesn't mean that you missed it for all times sake. Go back to the month you missed and call it forward to now and in the future. The Lord demonstrates great mercy, the type that is purposed to bless you even when you're not worthy to receive it. Case in point, He extended to you and me the gift of salvation through His precious Son Jesus the Christ. I'm sure you will agree none of us are worthy to receive such a precious gift! So call upon His mercy and ask forgiveness for any unholy acts. Be assured that the Lord will cleanse you as He fills you with His presence. In particular, this is the season that He will repair what is broken. If it's fixable, the Lord will tell you and He'll give you the plan to fix it. If He doesn't tell you to fix it, let go and let it die, so this is the time to lay down unsanctified mercy and pride in particular!

It's also the mother month, a nurturing time in which the loving touch of the Lord will gently guide and help you, it's also an apostolic month; it's the season to see who is fathering you. It's the time to remember that there is strength greater than you. In other words you do not have to be strong all the time, "Allow the Lord to be your strength."

Additionally, because Gad is the tribe that is associated with Elul this is a very prophetic month. Permit the Lord to speak into your heart and those whom the Lord has placed over you to speak into your life. Listen intently to the prophetic voice because it may come as a whisper. Also because the God of peace reigns in your heart you must function in that peace. It's the month for the inner knowledge of peace to be activated. It's through peace that God gives us the time to realign. So petition the Lord to place deep within your heart a peace that passes all understanding, and He will give it to you.

Elul is the month in which complex issues are worked out, so if there is a problem in your life that just doesn't seem to go away, petition the Lord for an answer. This is the month where you either birth blessings or birth something God is going to hate later on, so be very careful what you birth. If your birthing was brought forth from a wrong disposition you will reap the whirlwind of it later on. So be sure your emotions are functioning at proper spiritual levels. Furthermore, don't allow your emotions to drive you, surrender them to the Holy Spirit. Remember to make decisions when you are calm, rather than from a tumultuous perspective. Ask for counsel and make decisions while you're cool, calm and collected. Another important point is to take the focus off yourself and place it on others.

As the month of Elul draws to a close, the mood of repentance should become more urgent in the Spirit. Prayers for forgiveness may increase. A fundamental part of Prayers of Forgiveness is recognizing the Lord's thirteen attributes of mercy that were revealed to Moses after the sin of the Golden Calf (Exodus 34:6-7). The attributes are: 1) Ha-shem (<u>God</u>), 2) Ha-shem (<u>God</u>), 3) <u>God,</u> 4) <u>Merciful</u>, 5) <u>Gracious</u>, 6) <u>Long-suffering</u>, 7) <u>Abundant in goodness</u>, 8) <u>Truth</u>, 9) <u>Keeping mercy unto the thousandth generation</u>, 10) <u>Forgiving iniquity</u>, 11) <u>Transgression</u>, 12) <u>Sin</u> and 13) <u>One who cleanses</u>. Why are there three attributes named God? Different names of God connote different characteristics of Him. The Name rendered as "Ha-shem is the name used when God is exhibiting characteristics of mercy, and it is said that this dual usage indicates <u>that the Lord is merciful before a person sins</u>, but is <u>also merciful after a person sins</u>. The third attribute is a different Name of God that is used when He acts in His capacity as the Almighty Ruler of nature and the universe.

King David said: "…that I may <u>dwell</u> in the house of the Lord all the days of my life, to behold the beauty of the Lord, and to frequent God's temple" (Psalm 27:4). There is an apparent contradiction here, "dwell" has a sense of permanency about it but "to frequent" implies a measure of transience. King David's desire was to dwell in the house of the Lord on a permanent basis all the days of his life, but since permanent dwelling can be tainted with suspicion of habit and routine, he further requested "to frequent." A person who comes to visit frequently has a taste of something new each time. And so King David's request was to be a permanent resident in the house of the Lord, but with a level of constant renewal as though he were visiting frequently, as though he were coming to visit anew, God's temple. During the month of Elul our primary passion is to put right any area where we are disconnected from the Lord so His presence can dwell with us!

The purpose of this month is to bring you into the Presence of the Lord by renewing your relationship with Him. Let nothing rob you of that privilege, in Jesus Name!

The Gate of Repentance
PROPHETIC DECLARATIONS

<u>**Declare prophetically over your life, church, and the seven spheres of influence that:**</u>

- The Gate of Repentance is opened.
- Repentance is made for sinful activity.
- Mistrust is being healed.
- Connection with God's window of opportunity occurs.
- Charitable giving is practiced.
- Relationship with the Lord is recaptured.
- Spiritual complacency is broken and passion arises.
- Wrongs that have been committed against others are forgiven.
- Attitudes align with the principles of the kingdom of God.
- Reward is received for good spiritual work.
- Burdens are given to the Lord.
- The wonder of God is experienced to release an outpouring.
- The mercy of God is received.
- The nurturing touch of the Lord is accepted.
- The Lord is my strength.
- The Lord is speaking into lives and they are responding.
- God's peace is received.

- The Lord is solving complex issues.
- Emotions are surrendered to the Holy Spirit and spiritual alignment occurs.

"In order to transform our environment we <u>must</u> change."

Scripture References

Exodus 32, 34:6-7, 34:27-28
Song of Solomon 6:3
Mark 11:25
Matthew 11:28-30

Prayer Proclamations

<u>Acts 3:19</u> "Repent, then, and turn to God, so that your sins may be wiped out, <u>that times of refreshing may come from the Lord</u>."

<u>Isaiah 57:15</u> "I live in a high and holy place, but also with him who is contrite and lowly in spirit, to revive the spirit of the lowly and to revive the heart of the contrite."

****

<u>PRAY THAT</u>:
- We ask the Lord to transform our hearts
- Through repentance we experience a true change in behavior (Ezekiel 18:31; Acts 17:30)
- As we repent we will experience increased passion and obedience to the Lord (II Chronicles 7:14)
- We trust and partner with God's desire to move us deeper into relationship with Him (Joel 2:13)
- We are willing to receive God's mercy and forgiveness (Isaiah 30:18, 55:7)
- We are willing to move beyond sin into His refreshing (Acts 3:19)
- As we recognize and release what has come between us and God, we will experience true life (Ezekiel 18:21)

REPENT and REFUSE TO PARTNER WITH:

- Refusal to quit sinning
- Isolating/Refusing to listen to the Holy Spirit's direction
- Complacency / Ingratitude for forgiveness
- Fear of what God wants to change in our life
- Pride that keeps us focused on the sin, not Jesus' forgiveness
- Settling for the status quo
- Love of sin more than love of God

****

***II Corinthians 7:10** "Godly sorrow brings repentance that leads to salvation <u>and leaves no regret</u>, but worldly sorrow brings death."*

Chapter Twelve

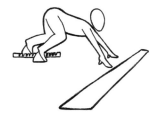

The Gate of New Beginnings

"I will give you a new heart and put a new spirit in you; I will remove from you your heart of stone and give you a heart of flesh."
~ Ezekiel 36:26

OVERVIEW

According to Hebraic custom "Tishri" is the seventh month (I Kings 8:2) on the Jewish calendar. It begins in September and ends in October on our Gregorian calendar. The tribe associated with this month is "Ephraim," and it means to be "fruitful and multiply." It's the satiated or satisfied fully month, because there are four major holy days that are observed by the Jewish people. The Holy days are "Rosh Hashanah," "The Ten Days of Awe," "Yom Kippur" and the "Feast of Tabernacles."

GENERAL INFORMATION

As it applies to Tishri, the gate name for this month is "New Beginnings" because according to Jewish custom it is "The head of the year" or "The first of the year." From a biblical perspective

Rosh Hashanah is the Jewish New Year and the Hebraic calendar changes. Truly this is the season for "New Beginnings!"

New Beginnings is quite different in the eyes of a Spirit-led Christian; it becomes a spiritual reality rather than a human passion. Moreover, the key to walk in New Beginnings is to humble yourself to <u>listen</u>, <u>embrace</u> and <u>carry out</u> God's directives. It's a spiritual walk that causes the favor of the Lord to come upon you!

New Beginnings speaks of newness; it implies that the Lord has given you a "do over." From a spiritual perspective New Beginnings occur when the Holy Spirit renews you daily as you are led about by faith in Him! So during this season ask the Lord to redeem your time, life, faith, school, church and city granting a fresh start, leaving behind those things that have, in the past, negatively influenced you. This is the time to forget past issues that have brought an absence of life and press into what the Lord has for you now and in the future! Because the four Festivals are important and everlasting (Numbers 10:8; Leviticus 16:29-31, 23:41-42; John 7:37-38), we as Christians, should realize their significance without establishing legalistic and ritualistic patterns which represent the religious system. Since you and I know Jesus we have the privilege to experience these important days from a spiritual perspective causing these celebrations to be truly extraordinary! We should rid ourselves of fear of tradition and erroneous teachings regarding these holy days, and welcome them into our Christian experience. These holy days reveal the heart of the Lord for the church and all of mankind. The proper way to celebrate these festivals is to follow the leading of the Holy Spirit, and align with Christ.

Rosh Hashanah is the Feast of Trumpets. It's a wake-up call; a time set by God to call you to attention. Rosh Hashanah is the head of the year (Leviticus 23:24).

The Ten Days of Awe is an extended time of seeking the Lord. The "Ten Days of Awe," is also called days of "Teshuvah." Teshuvah is a Hebrew word that means "to turn" and "to return." It means repentance, but it is also a word for springtime. When God gives you a wakeup call (Rosh Hashanah) quickly turn from anything that hinders your walk with the Lord and return to Him! You may have started the last year close to the Lord but ended up "drifting" and getting off course. You may have neglected key appointments with Him causing you to be ensnared by sin. This ten day period is part of the Lord's countdown to glory.

If you have listened to the trumpet blast (Rosh Hashanah), something has awakened in your spirit. The response should be a time of seriously seeking the Lord. You may, during this time, praise Him and delve deeper in the word of God. You may also allow the Lord to reveal and heal old demonic cycles in your life. Let Him quicken your spirit and awaken a new level of love for Him! When you have diligently sought the Lord during the Days of Awe, you are ready for the Day of Atonement!

Yom Kippur is the Day of Atonement. It's a time for your fellowship with the Lord to be restored. It's known as the heart of the year.

The Feast of Tabernacles is an appointed time to

experience God's presence.

Prophetically

The fall feasts provide a pattern for revival for you, your family, church, city and nations. The Lord gave one commandment for the Festival of Trumpets (Rosh Hashanah); "All His people must listen to a blast of the trumpets! The blast of the shofar is a call to awaken! The Hebrew name for this feast is, Yom Teruah, and it means, "The day of the awakening blast!" We need a wakeup call to come to attention as we enter our new season. When you hear the blast of the shofar, ask the Lord to show you anything in your life that would hinder His work in you so that New Beginnings will happen. Tishri is known as the month of return, meaning those things that have been scattered will be restored. During this time you will see, as you submit to the Holy Spirit, resolution of issues. It's the season when you petition the Lord about what you've let the enemy scatter and through proper alignment see it return to you. While you're asking why not request a one hundred fold return?

It's during the month of Tishri that the Lord will cause judgments or blessings to be released as He weighs your deeds. That's why it's important to interact with Him daily ensuring that what is being judged today reverts to good and fruitful blessings tomorrow. Because the seventh month is linked to Joseph (Ephraim, Joseph's son), expect a double-portion released to you if you're in right alignment! If not then reposition yourself because this is the season to properly align to receive the double portion blessing. Nevertheless, this double portion may be in blessing or misfortune depending upon what or whom you've based your previous decisions on.

The wonderful thing about the Lord is that whatever you've done that was ungodly; repentance will redirect your course releasing New Beginnings for a double portion.

This is the month that bitterness can easily find its mark in your life. Bitterness defined means hard to bear, grievous, distressful, causing pain, piercing or stinging. It also means to be resentful or cynical. Ask the Lord to remove any type of evil that can open the door to this demonic activity. Bitterness opens the way for stress and infirmity. This is the month that you must be well balanced and in control of your spiritual and natural faculties. Be careful that you don't put in motion something that you will regret later! Ask the Lord to give you spiritual balance so that you can identify and correct the cause of bitterness now and in the future. The Lord wants you to see people through His eyes of compassion rather than through your eyes of offense!

The Holy Spirit must be preeminent in your life. You must stay under the influence of the Holy Spirit or demonic spirits will drive you to agree with the plans of darkness in the earth. There are certain changes in the earth that have occurred in the last several years that have created motion that cannot be stopped. The kingdom of darkness must give way to the kingdom of God that is advancing with new strength. The supernatural power of the Lord is being released on His people who are creating a dramatic spiritual change in the earth.

This is the month for touch, in particular touching the heart of the Lord just as the woman did in Matthew 9:18-22. As you press through things that distract and hold you captive you will experience Jesus' virtue just as the woman did. So be persistent this month and pursue the Lord until He answers you. Patience is a great attribute that you will need as you push through those difficulties that have kept you isolated from Him. Nevertheless, trials many times occur because the Lord is testing your resolve and watching to see if you'll press through any barrier that has kept you separated from Him.

Here are some other prophetic points to consider:

- There will be physical manifestations of what you have been watching and waiting to see this year!
- You will supernaturally transcend your limitations and begin a new period of interaction with the Lord.
- There will be an aligning of the land and heaven to create a new Divine presence in your life.
- Dominion will be the key word for you this year. Rule where you've been positioned. Be watchful that demonic forces do not gain ground on you during this time frame!
- This is the year that God's people will have a great authority over their enemies.
- All squatters must go from your inheritance or they will gain squatters rights and their encroachment will remain another season. Land in this case is equated to your mind, therefore, this year transform your mind so you can have victory!
- Be aggressive to overthrow all poverty mentalities! "A lion is on the road, I'll hide myself," should not be your theme. Stand firm and face anything that might try to trespass onto your territory that might try to obstruct you moving down your path.

- It's during Tishri that you must break your orphan spirit!
- Return to a place of innocence.
- Stay in the secret place because it's as you stay in this place that you can be sent forth on key missions for the Lord.

This is the time to forget past issues that have brought an absence of life and press into what the Lord has for you now and in the future!

Let's look at the last two observances of the month of Tishri, which are the Day of Atonement and the Feast of Tabernacles. The Day of Atonement answers the question, "How can we enjoy fellowship with a Holy God?" In the Old Testament, Yom Kippur was the day the High Priest entered the Holy of Holies to reconcile the breach that occurred between man and God in the Garden of Eden! The Bible teaches that you and I were created to dwell with God and He placed within us a hunger for His Presence. That's why, many times, we're unsatisfied, because we try to fill our emptiness with ungodly things. The one thing that restores our separation from God is atonement (another word for atonement is redemption). It's important during this season to acknowledge the power of Jesus' atoning blood. Separation from the Lord equals emptiness in our hearts and emptiness must be filled! So make sure you fill the void with the Lord.

When sin entered the world, we were cut off from the presence of the Lord. Our Heavenly Father hates sin; He hates what it does to us – the sickness, pain, suffering and loss that it produces in our lives. Sin is a violation of His character; it robs the Lord of our intimate relationship with Him. It's because of sin that man cannot come into the presence of the Lord. In Moses' Tabernacle and again in Solomon's Temple, a thick curtain called "The Veil" was used to separate the people from the place of God's presence. To restore fellowship, sin has to be covered and that's what atonement does! Aren't you thankful that the Blood of Jesus covers our sins?

Prophetically

The Day of Atonement or Yom Kippur is the heartbeat of the year. It's the day of forgiveness and reconciliation where you can fearlessly enter the forest within yourself to explore the deepest parts of your life, the areas that are too dark for you to see or even want to see. When you earnestly examine yourself, you will find that you may have blocked your ability to be a spiritual person because of life's superficial (shallow) side. No one is perfect and in truth one of the greatest problems that each of us faces is that we have fooled ourselves into believing we need to be perfect. We all have a tendency to rationalize, reframe and deny away our spiritual and moral failures. It's during the Day of Atonement that the Lord helps you break denial! So deliverance during Yom Kippur is particularly important for your healing!

As you look inside yourself, you will see there is goodness and a yearning for the Lord. Therefore, the Day of Atonement is the time to pull back the curtains of your life, and see yourself not as you have become, but as He has destined you to be! You will never be able to achieve this dimension of redefinition on your own. Yom Kippur is the time the Lord releases His Holy pressure to open doors for you. The truth is you must be brave enough to walk through the doors that God opens. For those of you who choose to walk through the threshold, extreme blessing will greet you!

Many Christians have never experienced the blessing of really <u>confessing their sins</u>. They've never known the peace that comes when you know that you're completely free of all guilt. In fact many Christians may have never really confessed their sins at all! As a result, they have so much rage, disappointment and guilt they wouldn't know how to begin to confess them even if they tried. Several years ago a pastor asked his congregation a question during the Sunday service, "How many of you have sinned already this morning?" <u>Every</u> hand went up, the pastor then asked, "How many of you know what sin you committed?" Ninety-five per cent of the hands went down. Only a handful of people knew the sin that they had committed <u>the rest just felt guilty</u>! Many Christians live most of their lives filled with guilt. If you feel guilty, but don't know how to address this issue, I have good news for you. During this season of atonement God wants you to experience the reality of His forgiveness through Jesus Christ; guilt can stop you from moving forward just as unconfessed sin does! You can correct your position (alignment) by allotting time to spend with the Lord. Ask Him to reveal sins and feelings of guilt that you need to confess and then write them down. When you're finished with the list, confess them openly to Him repenting over each sinful act or guilty feeling. Then wad up the paper and throw it away, because that's exactly what the Lord did when you confessed and repented.

The culmination of God's cycle of blessing during Tishri is

found in the Feast of Tabernacles. A Tabernacle, or Sukkot, is an appointed time to come boldly into His presence, knowing that every hindrance is removed; it's a time to experience God's Glory and a time to joyfully fellowship with Him!

During the Feast of Tabernacles the Lord's Glory is the tangible manifestation of His presence. God is omnipresent, but there are certain times when His presence is revealed in ways that are discernable to our five senses. So anytime you're experiencing the Lord's presence in a palpable way you're encountering His Glory. When His Glory comes everything changes! You'll find salvation, repentance, empowering transformation, healing, provision, miracles and fulfillment, to say the least. During Tabernacles (Sukkot) expect to experience His Glory!

Therefore, a powerful aspect of the Feast of Tabernacles is to celebrate God's Glory. During Tabernacles, shout out to the Lord for a fresh outpouring of His splendor. Because Rosh Hashanah, the Ten Days of Awe, the Day of Atonement and the Feast of Tabernacles are guidelines for revival (a reforming move of the Spirit), ask the Lord to revive and reform you, His Church and all man-kind!

Every year, during the Feast of Tabernacles, the High Priest performed a prophetic act. He would bring water from the pool of Siloam, carry it up to the temple and pour it out beside the altar. This symbolized an appeal to God for the latter rain to fall on the land. It also symbolized an appeal for the outpouring of His Spirit, the "spiritual rain" spoken of in Joel chapter two. This action of the pouring out of the water from Siloam was repeated everyday of the feast. When they came to the last day commonly known as the "Great Day," of the feast the priest brought water from the pool of Siloam and huge crowds would have accompanied him. The temple court would have been packed with people anxious to watch this important ceremony. As the priest stood beside the altar this particular day, a hush fell over the crowd. According to John 7:37-38, as the priest was preparing to pour the water beside the altar, Jesus stood and cried out in loud voice, "If any man is thirsty, let him come to Me and drink. He who believes in me, from his innermost being shall flow rivers of living water." That's what the Lord wants for every one of us; He wants us to experience His living waters. So the celebration of the feasts culminating with Sukkot is a season of preparation to experience the Lord at greater degrees. That's why it's important to recognize these holy days allowing them to fit comfortably into your Christian experience. Anything that enhances your relationship with the Lord should be incorporated in your life!

The Feast of Tabernacles is an appointed time with the Lord. Missing that time is not a sin; honestly the Lord doesn't want this fellowship to become legalistic. It's not about getting every detail of the celebration right; it's a matter of meeting the Lord. Relating with the Lord enables us to resonate His life and timing. When you are in rhythm with God you are out of sync with satan. When you're on the same wave length as the Lord you cut off the enemies strategies and it holds you from drifting from God. It keeps you in right alignment for passing through the windows of opportunity and it always brings you to new levels in the Lord. Please be encouraged to enter in and stay in God's Holy cycle where you will discover abundant life.

The original ceremony for the Day of Atonement involved two goats. The first goat was called "The goat of the Lord." The High Priest would slaughter and sprinkle its blood on the mercy seat making atonement (redemption). The second goat was called the "scapegoat," it was a goat for the sins of the people. The High Priest would lay both hands on the head of the live goat and confess over it all the wickedness and rebellion of the Israelites, all their sins, putting them on the goats head. Then the goat was released to roam in the desert. This was a tangible picture to the Jews that their sin was removed (Leviticus 16: 15-22).

Furthermore, for centuries God gave His people another visible sign of their atonement. It was a Jewish custom to tie a red sash to the door of the Temple each year on the Day of Atonement. When the Lord accepted the sacrifice, **the red sash turned white**, this took place year after year. According to the Jewish Talmud something alarming happened forty years before the destruction of the Temple in 70 A.D. In the year A.D. 30 **the red sash stopped turning white**, God no longer accepted the sacrifice of atonement! Why did the sash stop turning white in A.D. 30? It's because in that year, Jesus was sacrificed in Jerusalem! The offering of God's perfect sacrifice made the yearly oblation of a goat unnecessary. Jesus became the atoning sacrifice. His Blood atoned for our sins, past, present and future. Through that precious act you and I have been released to have fellowship with the Lord once again!

The last holy day of Tishri is the Feast of Tabernacles; it's a celebration of God's Glory. This festival is a season to remember past experiences of His splendor, a time to seek His face and experience His Glory today and everyday; it's also the season to call out to God for a fresh outpouring of His Glory during this New Year. Moreover, these holy days are a period to enjoy the Lord and celebrate His goodness. Leviticus 23:40 says, "Rejoice before the Lord your God for seven days." Deuteronomy 16:14-15 says, "Be joyful at your feast, for the Lord your God will bless you and your joy will be complete."

In the Bible, there are actually five tabernacles where God's Glory was and is manifested. In a broad sense this feast celebrates all five of these tabernacles, they are: The Tabernacle of Moses, of David, of Jesus, the Eternal Tabernacle and the Tabernacle of the Church. All five of these tabernacles have this in common, that God's presence and His Glory dwelt with men. It was in these Holy places that the Lord released His blessings to His people. That's what the Feast of Tabernacles celebrates, God's precious glory being released to His people!

Therefore, the Feast of Tabernacles is a time to celebrate that God tabernacles (interacts) with His people. He wants His Glory to be a part of your life. He tabernacled (interacted) with Israel in the wilderness, He tabernacled (interacted) on earth with Jesus and He continues to relate with us today through the power of His Holy Spirit! We need to call out to the Lord for His Glory to come and dwell with us changing us into His likeness!

The Gate of New Beginnings
PROPHETIC DECLARATIONS

<u>*Declare prophetically over your life, church, and the seven spheres of influence that*</u>:

- The Gate of New Beginnings is opened.
- The Lord is awakening souls.
- All will turn and then return to the Lord through repentance.
- The Ten Days of Awe is a countdown to God's Glory.
- All will praise the Lord and delve deeper into the Bible.
- The Lord is healing old wounds and sinful cycles.
- The Lord returns everything that satan has scattered or stolen.
- A double portion of spiritual and natural blessings is received.
- Bitterness is released.
- The Lord brings spiritual balance.
- Israel will experience peace!
- Emptiness will be filled with God's presence.
- Seeking the Lord's face releases a fresh outpouring of His Glory.
- God is interacting (to tabernacle) with us.
- Destiny is in Jesus.

- Spiritual transformation and joyful fellowship leads to a new dimension in Christ.
- Recognition of bondage leads to freedom.
- God's appointed time to resonate His life will be received.
- The Lord is demolishing the strategy of the enemy.

"In order to transform our environment we <u>must</u> change."

Scripture References

Psalm 122
Isaiah 62

PRAYER PROCLAMATIONS

<u>I Kings 18:30</u> *"Then Elijah said to all the people, 'Come here to me.' They came to him, and he repaired the altar of the Lord, which was in ruins."*

****

<u>PRAY THAT</u>:
- We ask the Lord to transform our hearts
- We walk in humility recognizing the need for change (I John 1:8)
- We are in right alignment walking in God's direction (Psalm 48:14; Isaiah 30:21, 45:2)
- We are diligent and have a willingness to work (I Kings 18:30-37)
- We are walking in radical obedience (I Samuel 15:22)
- Everything the enemy has stolen is being restored (Joel 2:25)
- Bitterness be removed from our lives and the door to infirmity is shut (Ephesians 4:31-32)
- We have a desire for God above <u>anything</u> (Matthew 22:37-41)

<u>REPENT and REFUSE TO PARTNER WITH</u>:
- Pride/Deception – Believing we are sinless
- Rebellion – Following our own desires instead of leadership
- Selfishness – Refusal to give up our time or effort for God's work

- Disobedience – Refusal to do as God asks/directs
- Hardening my heart – Refusal to listen to the Holy Spirit
- Luke warmness – Neither hot nor cold

****

II Chronicles 7:1 *"When Solomon finished praying, fire came down from heaven and consumed the burnt offering and the sacrifices, and the glory of the Lord filled the temple."*

II Chronicles 7:15-16 *" Now my eyes will be open and my ears attentive to the prayers offered in this place … My eyes and my heart will always be there."*

Chapter Thirteen

The Gate of Deliverance

"No temptation has seized you except what is common to man. And God is faithful; he will not let you be tempted beyond what you can bear. But when you are tempted, he will also provide a way out so that you can stand up under it."
~ I Corinthians 10:13

OVERVIEW

According to Hebraic custom the <u>eighth month</u> on the Jewish calendar is "<u>Cheshvan</u>" characterized as Bul in I Kings 6:38 and it begins in October and ends in November on the Gregorian calendar. The tribe associated with this month is "<u>Manasseh</u>" and it signifies that you should "<u>Forget</u>." The gate name is "The Gate of <u>Deliverance</u>." During this month you should petition the Lord to deliver you from bondages asking Him to help you "forget" them.

GENERAL INFORMATION

From a Christian perspective your walk of faith must be

matched with Christ like behavior and lifestyle, you can't live a double standard claiming to be led of Christ. Perhaps you've asked what deliverance means and what is the process? First, it's acknowledging that you're operating in an ungodly attitude or sinful behavior. Then you ask the Lord to remove any bondage and trust that He will do so. Next is the most important step, when you choose to partner with the Lord by taking responsibility and refusing to engage once again in your old unholy patterns. (Example – when we are delivered from addictions we must resist them every day by choosing to disregard our will). So deliverance is a weapon of war because it unlocks the shackles that the enemy has placed on you. Biblically, deliverance means picking up your cross, everyday and following Jesus (Matthew 16:24-26)! It's a daily process to properly align with the Lord against sinful activity, such as ungodly speech, wrong attitudes or evil desires. Through transparency, obedience and humility you can ask the Lord to liberate you from these ungodly activities and because of His love for you, He will!

Colossians 3:5-11 says, "Put to death, therefore, whatever belongs to your earthly nature: <u>sexual immorality</u> (habitual immorality), <u>impurity</u> (physical impurity), <u>lust</u> (uncontrolled desire), <u>evil desire and greed</u> (an evil desire for more), which is <u>idolatry</u>. Because of these, the wrath of God is coming. You used to walk in these ways, in the life you once lived. But now you must rid yourselves of such things as these: <u>anger</u> (sudden anger), <u>rage</u> (long lasting anger), <u>malice</u> (the viciousness of the mind which all individual vices spring), <u>slander</u> (foul speech) and <u>filthy language</u> (obscene language) from your lips. Do not lie to each other (bare false witness), since you have taken off your old self with its practices and have put on the new self, which is being renewed in the knowledge in the image of its creator. Here there is no Greek or Jew, circumcised or uncircumcised, slave or free, but Christ is all, and is in all." Other problem areas that are equally as damaging are issues of rejection, witchcraft, betrayal, abandonment, insecurities, vindictiveness, unforgiveness, elitism, racism and the like. The language used in Colossians says to, "Put to Death," and is derived from the verb nekrosate, meaning literally "To make Dead!" It suggests that you are not to simply suppress or control evil acts and attitudes you are to "slay utterly," your old sinful way of living! To "slay utterly," means you must become aggressive about whatever binds you to that old lifestyle. This means that you cannot "flirt" with sin, or allow it to revisit you. You must put it under the Blood of Jesus and <u>LEAVE</u> it there!

C.D.F. Moule says it like this: "Christians must kill (put to death) self-centeredness and regard as dead all private desires and ambitions. There must be in his life a radical transformation of the will and a radical shift of the center of Christ. Everything, which would keep a Christian from obeying God and fully surrendering to the Lord, must be surgically (meaning deliverance) excised!" Deliverance is surrendering to the Lord, agreeing that something is standing between you and God. It's allowing Him to remove with your partnership whatever hindrance exists. It is important that you accept God's hand of deliverance as a normal part of your Christian experience. Dear ones, deliverance brings breakthrough!

Prophetically

There are times when the best way to serve God is to look deeply within yourself allowing Him to provide you with His anointings that move you forward in Him. There are other times in which the best way to minister to the Lord is by getting out of that warm bed, taking a shower, getting dressed, saying a prayer and facing the issues of the world with the help of the Holy Spirit. During this month you will need to take a deep breath and say, "<u>The time is now</u>!" All of the hopes, prayers and aspirations in which you see yourself clearly committed to grow spiritually must be set in concrete, in other words you have to see to it that your checks don't bounce! So during the month of Cheshvan you're accountable for who you are in the Lord, excuses don't hold water!

This is the month in which the great flood took place, it's that period in which destruction, nothing like the world has ever seen, occurred and it's the same season of rebirth and renewal, when the waters from the flood subsided and new life bursts forth. It was evil that caused the world's worst disaster, not inadequacy, not ugliness, but something far worse, evil is what reduces humans to an animal like state, and diminishes God's Kingdom to being nothing more than a semblance of the real. The downward spiral that led to the Flood is disturbingly familiar. For example, the first step toward devastation was relating to women as pleasure objects, does this sound familiar! The Bible tells us, "The men who were Godlike (meaning powerful) took any woman they wanted (including married women) and to justify their actions they created systems of religious beliefs in which God was reduced to a bigger version of them (similar to

Greek mythology)." During Cheshvan you need to examine yourself to see if you've also diminished the Lord by creating religious systems in order to justify sin.

Humans are defined by the act of <u>being</u>, thus human being! Once you forget "being" and adapt (become adjusted to new conditions) yourself to "having" as your supreme value, then you're no longer "good." The aftermath of the Flood reintroduced the concept of humans being human. The only survivor (other than his immediate family) is described as a righteous man and Noah is called "whole" or "simple." The way the Torah uses the word "simple" when describing Noah is the same way a chemist uses the word "simple" – he is what he is without additions or mixture! He was gloriously true to his archetype (original model which others can follow); he was a human that was about being. Are you a human that is being (going after) God's heart or one that is being (going after) your own (having)? The answer to this question is that you were put in this physical world with all of its temptations to be a candle in a dark place letting the goodness that it reflects illuminate the entire earth that you represent.

In Cheshvan you have choices to make about your relationship to the real world and to God's Kingdom. You have to make commitments to not flinch in the face of the mundane things that are set before you, and make dynamic choices in the Lord. Therefore, Cheshvan is a time of great opportunity; it's the month that you should yell "I'm Satisfied," pushing out everything that is dissatisfying to you. So be tenacious to guard against any negative activity in your life!

Cheshvan is the month of the sense of smell. In particular it's the season to smell the awesomeness of the Lord! May the fragrance of the Holy Spirit begin to come into your inner-man and into your surroundings! Historically, all of the sacrifices in the Temple service were meant to produce a "satisfying aroma" pleasing the Lord's sense of smell, which implies the Divine "satisfaction" with the service of His children and with His creation in general. This Divine satisfaction with man and creation was first expressed on the 28th of Cheshvan, when Noah offered his sacrifice to the Lord. Due to his sacrifice, God swore to Noah never again to destroy the world by flood and that the rainbow was the sign of that promise.

As is expressed in the Levitical laws of the Bible, it's the fats of the intestines that when offered on the altar produces the satisfying aroma for the Lord. The Lord will go deep into your life this month to deliver you of those things that separate you from His presence. Look for those things that are unnatural to the kingdom of God to burn during this season making a sweet aroma to arise into the nostrils of the Divine! Cheshvan is the month where the fragrance of the Lord will permeate your inner self by allowing the purifying process of His presence to occupy you. That said, you should prepare, especially this month, for a move of the Holy Spirit! You will need to permit the Lord to deal with your demonic root systems by embracing deliverance. Remember the Lord loves the smell of burning flesh!

This is the month to receive a new anointing that will break the oppression of satan and his minions. Without a new anointing satan gets an upper hand, so through receiving this impartation you're literally placing your heel on the neck of the enemy and his plans. This is the month that you pray and prophesy against the enemy's plans to stop or block your forward momentum. Furthermore, it's the season the Lord pulls you aside to examine your anointing to ensure you are using it properly. It's especially the time to deal with your mindsets, bondages, and hardships so that you're anointing can operate at its highest level. The truth is demonic mindsets and bondages hamper you from flowing in the anointing and must be dealt with in order to properly function, so it's the month to exchange your bondages for God's plan so He can transform you (deliverance). You will be transformed in a positive way through the guidance of the Holy Spirit, if not you'll continue to be bound by them at increased levels. Moreover, this is the month to forget your past issues of abandonment instead reflect fully upon God's plan for your life and His loving Father's heart!

During Cheshvan review the life of Moses. In particular examine how anger stopped the forward momentum of Moses and how it will stop you as well. So if you partner with anger or rage easily, allow the Lord to deliver you. Cheshvan is the month where the heavenlies will begin to produce strategies around you, opening the door for a greater presence of the Lord. Over and above, watch for deep and powerful revelations to be released during this time. Also know that you need a fresh anointing from the Lord because this is the month that you are to place your foot upon the neck of satan. Without fresh anointing you will produce negative results.

In reality, you need to cry out for God's anointing to press you through the pressures of life. Notwithstanding, this month you will be spiritually digesting the revelations that you have received in previous months. So allow God to work in your life!

Here are some additional points that are particularly important for Cheshvan:

- It's the month of Chodesh Bul, Mabul (the Flood lasting one year and ten days). *So the Lord deals with something until it is resolved*!

- It's the month the eternal flame of revelation moves you into a supernatural state. Watch for great revelation from the Lord!

- Since this is the month of the intestines it is the time for fine spiritual digesting of God's directives in your life. In reality you should be digesting revelatory things easily by now. So everything that you have received from the Lord in previous months should be clearly understood during Cheshvan.

- It's the month of the scorpion (venomous) such as the snake in the Garden of Eden. Be cautious that you are not bitten by the enticing words of the evil one.

- Cheshvan is the month of NUN. Though confined by boundaries of nature, light penetrates the darkness producing a new sound for the beginning.

You are not to simply suppress or control evil acts and attitudes you are to "slay utterly," your old sinful way of living! To "slay utterly," means you must become aggressive about whatever binds you to that old lifestyle and by doing so you will open "The Gate of Deliverance."

The Gate of Deliverance
PROPHETIC DECLARATIONS

<u>Declare prophetically over your life, church, and the seven spheres of influence that</u>:

- The Gate of Deliverance is opened.
- Who I am in the Lord is discovered.
- Systems are not created in order to justify sin.
- Choosing God's Kingdom over the world will cause me to cry out, "I am satisfied with the Lord."
- A guard is set against ungodly activity.
- The fragrance of God is welcome.
- Anything that separates me from the Lord is removed.
- Preparation is made for a move of the Holy Spirit.
- The enemy cannot stop forward spiritual momentum.
- Bondages are exchanged for God's plan so transformation can occur.
- The Lord is delivering me from anger or rage.
- God's anointing presses me through the pressures of life.
- Great spiritual revelation is coming.
- The enticing words of satan are not effective.
- God's light permeates the darkness of the societal gates.
- The supply lines are open and therefore the blessings of God are on their way!

"In order to transform our environment we <u>must</u> change."

Scripture References

Matthew 16:24-26
Colossians 3:5-11

PRAYER PROCLAMATIONS

<u>Matthew 16:25</u> *"If you try to keep your life for yourself, you will lose it. But if you give up your life for me, you will find true life."*

<u>1 John 3:6</u> *"No one who lives in him keeps on sinning. No one who continues to sin has either seen him or known him."*

****

PRAY THAT:
- We ask the Lord to transform our hearts
- We put to death our fleshly nature (Colossians 3:5-11; I John 3:6)
- We are willing to hear God's heart throb for us (Mark 10:21)
- We always follow Jesus' example (John 13:14, 15:5-10)
- We shift our will into Christ (Matthew 7:21; Luke 14:33)
- We see the truth about ourselves (John 8:31-36)
- We are becoming more productive in the kingdom (John 12:24)
- We are in total submission to the Lord (I Samuel 15:22; John 21:15)

REPENT and REFUSE TO PARTNER WITH:
- Sin in any form
- Loving earthly relationships more than Jesus
- Mammon – love of money/possessions
- Selfishness/Serving self
- Double-mindedness/partial submission

- Denial of sin/Covering sin
- Rebellion - Holding onto our life above the kingdom

Philippians 3:8-9 *"Everything else is worthless when compared with the priceless gain of knowing Christ Jesus my Lord. I have discarded everything else, counting it all as garbage, so that I may have Christ and become one with him."*

Chapter Fourteen

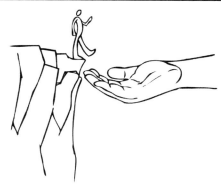

The Gate of Faithfulness

"Know therefore that the Lord your God is God; he is the faithful God, keeping his covenant of love to a thousand generations of those who love Him and keep His commands."
~ Deuteronomy 7:9

OVERVIEW

According to Hebraic custom the ninth month on the Jewish calendar is "Kislev" (Ezra 10:9) and it begins in November and ends in December on the Gregorian calendar. The tribe associated with this month is "Benjamin" meaning "the most gifted with the art of the bow." The tribe of Benjamin was known for their unwavering faith in God and their ferocious ability to battle evil. The gate name is "The Gate of Faithfulness."

GENERAL INFORMATION

The word faithful means steadfast, dedicated, dependable, obedient and worthy of trust. It's derived from the Hebrew root meaning "to trust (a person)," or "to believe (a statement)." This is the same definition that gives us the word "amen" (so be it). The distinction is that the one so described is trustworthy, dependable, trusting or loyal. For example, Moses was faithful in all God's household (Numbers 12:7), and "faithful" is used to describe the relation of God and Israel (Deuteronomy 7:9), as well as our faithful God keeps His covenant, and faithful people keep His commandments.

Faithfulness becomes the catalyst that perpetuates mastery. To be faithful one should go on resolutely in spite of opposition, meaning you must learn to "persevere." To persevere is to be given a task and achieve it in spite of difficulties, opposition or discouragement; it means to stay the course even if the odds feel overwhelming. Remember, "When things get tough, 'it's the rubbing that brings out the shine' and a person who is faithful, takes what has been given him and creates sweet victory from it!"

In the New Testament the adjective "faithful" is a derivative of the Greek noun meaning "faith" and it's here that we get the translation "faithful" as a natural offshoot of faith. The basic thought is that one has fidelity (continuing faithfulness to a person, cause or belief) toward the Lord and others. For example, in I Corinthians 7:25 Paul commended himself to the Corinthians as one who is "faithful" (KJV) or "trustworthy" (NAS). In Revelation 2:10 the church in Smyrna is commanded "be faithful unto death." In Ephesians 1:1 Paul addressed his letter "to the faithful in Christ Jesus." In other cases, however, "faithful" describes God's manner of relation toward His creation.

Many times God speaks as one who is faithful in order to comfort and encourage Christians. For example, "If we confess our sins, He is <u>faithful</u> and just to forgive us our sins and purify us from all unrighteousness" (I John 1:9). "…And God is <u>faithful</u>; he will not let you be tempted beyond what you can bear…" (I Corinthians 10:13). "The one who calls you is <u>faithful</u> and he will do it" (I Thessalonians 5:24). The Lord's faithfulness should be so deeply reflected in the lives of His people that they be called simply "the faithful" (Psalm 31:23). The faithful person is steadfast, unchanging toward their faithfulness to God, and thoroughly grounded in relation to Him. This sort of fidelity is used in both the Old and New Testaments to describe God's relation to the world and the quality of relationship that Christians are called upon to have toward the Lord and with one another.

Vance Havner says this about faithfulness. "God is faithful and He expects His people to be faithful. God's word speaks of faithful servants, faithful in a few things, faithful in the least, faithful in the Lord, and in faithful ministers. And all points to that day when He will say, "Well done, My good and faithful servant." What terrible times we have in our churches trying to keep people faithful in attendance and loyal! How we reward, and picnic, coax and tantalize church members into doing things they don't want to do but, which they would do if they loved God! The only service that counts is faithful service. True faith shows up in faithfulness. Not everyone can sing or preach, but all can be faithful."

Prophetically

First and foremost Kislev, because of the influence of the

tribe of Benjamin (proficient with the bow), is a time where you are to shoot straight and move quickly in the Spirit, this is not the season to meander. Cut your losses and move on, listening intently to the Lord and obeying His directives by cutting off everything that hinders you! Moreover, the name Kislev is derived from the Hebrew word for "security" and "trust." There are two states of trust, one active and one passive, both of which are evident during this month. The miracle of Hanukkah reflects the <u>active trust</u> of which this festival was named. It's active because a small group of warriors fought against the Hellenistic Empire and won. The sense of sleep is the <u>passive trust</u> conveying that God's providence (the protective care of God) always guards over His children, even as we sleep.

During this month you must put into motion your <u>active trust</u> and rest in <u>passive trust</u> as you allow the Lord to mature and strengthen your walk in Him. It's the month of Samekh, meaning to trust God to another level, and show great confidence in Him. So ask your Heavenly Father to increase your trust in Him as well as in the delegated authority that He's given you. This trust includes believing the best for your leaders and releasing any and all offenses that you may have in your heart toward them, past and present.

Furthermore, even though we ought to help one another everyday (servant hood); this is the month to lend a greater degree of support to God's people so they may accomplish the Lord's directives at a higher dimension! Because Benjamin is the tribe that's associated with Kislev it's a month you must warfare, meaning you need to rely upon the Lord through your faithfulness to release tactics to overcome satan's attacks

(Ephesians 6:1-18)! While this is important for you to do everyday there is a greater release of prophetic warfare this season. So earnestly and strategically pray asking the Holy Spirit for insight about sensitive spiritual issues. Moreover, if you don't develop trust and confidence you may very well have to go around the process of the mountain experience until you do.

Because Benjamin is the tribe that's associated with Kislev it's a month you must warfare, meaning you need to rely upon the Lord through your faithfulness to release tactics to overcome satan's attacks (Ephesians 6:1-18)! While this is important for you to do everyday there is a greater release of prophetic warfare during this season. So earnestly and strategically pray asking the Holy Spirit for insight about sensitive spiritual issues. It's time to intercede (pray) spiritually against evil empires and cultures. In particular ask the Lord to give you insight about what you should pray regarding your city, state and country then stand with God against the darkness.

Kislev is the time when the covenant of the rainbow was reached, meaning, you need to be faithful to war in the Spirit until you have victory just like Noah stayed in the Ark until the Lord told him to exit it. It's also confirmation that when you go through something difficult, the Lord says to you that you won't go through that situation again!

It's important to gain spiritual insight about how to pray for the nation of Israel; you should warfare for the Jewish people's existence. So be faithful in your walk with the Lord aligning with Him in prayer and see Him accomplish powerful suddenlies that will strengthen your faith and determination! Kislev is the month of tranquility and peace, you must know that warfare is not chaos around you all the time; it's also about having peace in the midst of war. As you petition the Lord, know that great serenity will come over you "…And the peace of God, which transcends all understanding, will guard your hearts and your minds…" (Philippians 4:7) even as you destroy forces that are intent on demolishing everything they touch. You also need to enter a greater level of rest in the Lord allowing Him to navigate you through the minefields of life as you methodically and meticulously follow Him.

Kislev is the season for increased dreams and for your future to be revealed and placed in proper alignment. During this time you'll find that your interaction with the Lord will increase, so expect night visions, spiritual insight and other forms of spiritual exchange to occur (angelic visitation, hunger to pray, passion for God's Word, a deep desire to connect with the Body of Christ and a fervency to serve). Dreams are one way God communicates with us, because issues during the day have a tendency to interrupt our communication stream with Him. So be proactive to write out your dreams and ask the Lord to reveal their meaning. Be sensitive to the voice of the Lord and be careful you do not discount it because it came in an unusual way.

Furthermore, during this month you will need to investigate why you're having interrupted sleep patterns and ask the Lord to help you deal with them. You can start the healing process of interrupted sleep patterns by recognizing the Lord's Divine providence and His omnipotence.

The Holiday of Hanukkah is celebrated this month. Unlike Passover and Yom Kippur, which were biblical holidays that God gave to Moses on Sinai, Chanukah (Hanukkah) is a relatively new holiday, dating back to 165 B.C. It's not mentioned in the Jewish Bible, as it commemorates an event that took place during the time between the closing of the Tanakh (the Old Testament) and the writing of the New Covenant Scriptures (the New Testament). By the time of Jesus, Hanukkah had become a regular holiday, as is mentioned in the Gospel of John 10:22-30, "Then came the Feast of Dedication (i.e. Hanukkah) at Jerusalem. It was winter, and Jesus was in the temple area walking in Solomon's colonnade."

The word "Hanukkah" actually means dedication, and refers to the rededication of the Temple on 25 Kislev 165 B.C., after it had been desecrated by the Syrian King Antiochus Epiphanes. Antiochus attempted to force his own Greek culture and pagan religion on the people of Judea, going as far as to erect an altar of Zeus in the Holy Temple, and even sacrificing a pig on the altar. Of course, the Jewish people were outraged, and staged a successful rebellion led by Judah Maccabee. When they sought to light the Temple's Menorah, they found only a single cruse of olive oil that had escaped contamination by the Greeks; miraculously, the one day supply burned eight days, until new oil could be prepared under conditions of ritual purity. To commemorate this miracle, the sages instituted the Festival of Hanukkah. As soon as the war was over, the Maccabees returned to Jerusalem and cleansed the Temple.

Afterward they held a service of dedication – the first Hanukkah! Spiritually, Hanukkah signifies that you must keep the spiritual light burning in your heart. It also indicates the presence of the Holy Spirit is vitally important for your spiritual maturity! So during this Festival allow the light of the Menorah to represent the presence of the Holy Spirit enlightening and guiding your life. Agree with the Lord any darkness that exists must be removed by the light of His Presence!

This is the month of the belly, meaning, "out of your bellies shall flow rivers of living waters" (John 7:37-38 KJV), it's the time when the Lord will assist you in building proper relationships with one another as well as with Him. Furthermore, it's the season to understand your next measure of interaction with Him by accepting a deeper realm of the river flow in your life. However, if your inner man isn't properly engaged or aligned with the Lord, you may not see His fullness in your life come to pass. You may want to use this time to ask the Lord to place you in right alignment with Him so you can receive the spiritual download that He wants to give you. Thus, to gain revelation about the river of the Lord read Ezekiel chapter forty-seven, because receiving the river of revelation from God's throne brings life and it more abundantly.

The prevailing words that accentuate this month are dedication, steadfastness, commitment and loyalty, all of these are derived from the word "faithful." During Kislev you must make a decision to become faithful to the Lord, your families, the church, God's people and His directives. It's easy to notice and emphasis the evil that is at work in and around us.

During this month pay close attention to what the Lord is saying and doing. In summary, Kislev is a critical time for receiving prophetic revelation to develop your warfare strategies for new beginnings. It's the season for trusting the Lord and expressing our great confidence in Him. During Kislev warfare until you have the victory! Also, pray for yourself, home, church, city, state, country and for the peace of Israel. Remember that in warfare you need peace demonstrating your trust in Him even during turmoil. It's the season for the river of God to touch every portion of your life allowing the deep things of the Holy Spirit to change your life. This is the month to hit the mark for the upcoming Year of New Beginnings! It's the season to listen to your dreams! Finally, keep your spiritual lamps trimmed and full of the oil of the Holy Spirit not allowing lethargy or passivity to affect your life. A profound statement was made by Mother Teresa. Senator Mark Hatfield asked her, "How can you bear the load without being crushed by it?" My dear Senator, retorted Mother Teresa, "<u>I am not called to be successful, but faithful</u>!"

The Gate of Faithfulness
PROPHETIC DECLARATIONS

<u>Declare prophetically over your life, church, and the seven spheres of influence that</u>:

- The Gate of Faithfulness is opened.
- The Holy Spirit is leading us.
- Everything that hinders is cut off.
- Trust and confidence in the Lord occurs.
- God's people are supported.
- The Holy Spirit provides insight about personal issues.
- Victory comes when faithfully seeking the Lord in prayer.
- There is peace in Israel.
- Peace remains in the midst of the battle.
- A greater level of interaction with the Lord is released.
- Divine providence and omnipotence of the Lord is in my midst.
- The spiritual light is burning in hearts.
- The Holy Spirit is important for spiritual maturity.
- The Holy Spirit is enlightening and guiding.
- Proper relationships with one another as well as the Lord are developing.
- The Lord brings right alignment with Him.

"In order to transform our environment we <u>must</u> change."

The Gate of Faithfulness

PRAYER PROCLAMATIONS

<u>John 4:34</u> *"My food, said Jesus, is to do the will of him who sent me and to finish his work."*

****

<u>PRAY THAT</u>:
- We ask the Lord to transform our hearts
- We have passion: "To do the will of him who sent me" (John 4:34)
- We have willingness: "To finish his work" (II Chronicles 15:12-15; John 4:34)
- We are faithful to keep our covenants with God (Deuteronomy 28:1-2, 15; Joshua 24:24-27; II Kings 11:17-18, 23:3; II Chronicles 15:12-15)
- There is a perfection of my will: Giving my heart to God (Proverbs 23:26; II Chronicles 15:12-15; Romans 12:1)
- We have a greater understanding of loyalty: Dedication to God's ways above our own (Proverbs 23:26)
- We rise up to higher levels of commitment and obedience: Keeping God's ways (Proverbs 23:26)

<u>REPENT and REFUSE TO PARTNER WITH</u>:
- Indifference toward God or man
- Resistance to follow the Holy Spirit's call
- Ignorance/Passivity regarding our covenants with God
- Isolation/Independence - Refusal to partner with God
- Rebellion - Choosing our way above God's
- Betrayal of our first love

****

<u>Proverbs 23:26</u> *"My son, give me your heart and let your eyes keep to my ways."*

<u>II Chronicles 15:12-15</u> *"They entered into a covenant to seek the Lord, the God of their fathers; with all their heart and soul … They sought God eagerly, and he was found by them."*

Chapter Fifteen

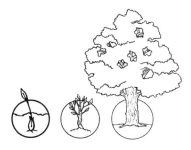

The Gate of Spiritual Maturity

"Then we will no longer be infants, tossed back and forth by the waves, and blown here and there by every wind of teaching and by the cunning and craftiness of men in their deceitful scheming."
~ Ephesians 4:14

OVERVIEW

According to Hebraic custom the <u>tenth month</u> (Esther 2:16) on the Jewish calendar is "<u>Tevet</u>" and it begins in December and ends in January on our Gregorian calendar. The tribe associated with the month is "<u>Dan</u>" meaning to "<u>judge, grow up and mature</u>." The tribe was known for engaging in the battle of holy anger against evil anger, which is maturity or they rose up to bite with the venom of anger, which is immaturity. The gate name is "The Gate of <u>Spiritual Maturity</u>."

GENERAL INFORMATION

The word "mature" means having attained a final or desired

state, being fully grown and developed. We all should be on a spiritual journey toward maturity in Christ. I encourage you to press forward toward the mark of spiritual development. It's easy to stay static (not moving) and satisfied where you are because of bondages of fear and laziness. Dear ones, maturity does have a price that many don't choose to pay.

There are many things that afflict the Body of Christ; there are two that I would like to bring to your attention. <u>First</u>, an apathetic attitude has encroached upon the lives of the Saints as it applies to spiritual development and <u>second</u>, spiritual dullness has produced a passionless pursuit of the Lord. These bondages yield immaturity, lethargy, indifference, religious attitudes (performance), and open the way for idolatry!
Therefore, Tevet is the month that you must individually answer the call of the Lord and stand against apathy and spiritual dullness. Hence, you must open and go through "The Gate of Spiritual Maturity."

Hebrews 5:11-14 says, "We have much to say about this, but it is hard to explain because you are slow to learn. In fact, though by this time you ought to be teachers, you need someone to teach you the elementary truths of God's word all over again. You need milk, not solid food! Anyone, who lives on milk, being still an infant, is not acquainted with the teachings about righteousness. But solid food is for the mature, who by constant use have trained themselves to distinguish between good and evil."

The writer to the Hebrews deals with the difficulties, which confront him in attempting to get across an adequate understanding of Christianity to his hearers. He's faced with two issues. First, the full orb of the Christian faith is by no means an easy thing to grasp nor can it be learned in a day. Second, the hearing of his listeners is spiritually dull. The word he uses (nothros) means slow-moving in mind, torpid (inactive and lacking in energy) in understanding, dull of hearing, and witlessly forgetful. It relates to the numbed limbs of an animal that is ill, or to a person who has the perceptive nature of a stone!

Hebrews 5:11-14 has something to say to everyone whose spiritual purpose it is to bring a life-giving message of the Gospel to people. It often happens that we as leadership reason ourselves out of teaching something because it's difficult or challenging. We then defend ourselves by saying that our hearers would never grasp it. It's truly a tragedy of the church that there is so little attempt to teach the deep things of God, or grasp the spiritual understanding and thought of the Lord's Kingdom.

It's true that ministering the deep things of God is difficult and that often means meeting the lethargy of the lazy mind and the embattled prejudice of the shut mind, however, the writer of Hebrews did not avoid bringing his message nor should we. Proclaiming the Gospel is designed to challenge and provoke you to good works. Many choose to listen to only what tickles their ears, rejecting the message that can bring them into right alignment with the Lord. When difficulties come it's easier to transfer blame to others feeling as though you have not been properly trained to meet the challenge, when in reality you were, you just chose not to apply what you were taught! The writer of Hebrews regarded it his supreme responsibility to pass on the truth that he knew! I too believe that one day the fullness of what the Lord has given you will saturate your spirit releasing revelation that will ultimately destroy those things that keep you lifeless! The complaint of the writer is that his hearers have been Christians for many years and are still babes no nearer maturity. The difference between the immature Christian and the child, between milk and solid food, often occurs in the New Testament (I Peter 2:2; I Corinthians 2:6, 3:2, 14:20; Ephesians 4:13). There are reasons for these analogies; the writer's are trying to cause their hearers to be stirred to newfound passions for the Lord.

According to Hebrews it says that by now they should be teachers. It's important that you don't take that literal, to say that a man was able to teach is a Greek way of saying that he had a grasp of the subject. The writer says that they still need someone to teach them the simple elements (stoicheia, a grasp of the subject) of Christianity. This word has a variety of meanings. In grammar it means the A B C's of the alphabet, in physics it means the four basic elements of which the world is composed. In philosophy it's the first elementary principles with which the student begins. It's the sorrow of the writer of Hebrews that after many years of Christianity his people have never got past the rudiments (fundamentals); they are like children who don't know the difference between right and wrong. Here he's face to face with a problem, which haunts the church in every generation <u>that of the Christian who refuses to grow up spiritually</u>!

Christians can refuse to grow up in spiritual knowledge. They are however, like a surgeon who refuses to use the new techniques of surgery, refuses to use the new anesthetics, refuses to use any new equipment and says: "What was good for Lister is good enough for me." They're like a physician who refuses to use any of the new drugs and says: "What I learned as a student fifty years ago is good enough for me." In religious things it's still worse. God is infinite; the riches of Christ are unsearchable; and you are missing out on the riches of who He is, along with the blessings of His powerful anointing. At the end of the day we should be steadily maturing in the ways of God.

Moreover, there are people who never mature in their behavior as well. It may be forgivable for a child to sulk or to be liable to fits of temper, but there are many adults who are as childish in their behavior. A case of arrested development is always a heart rendering thing; but it's even worse when Christians allow their spiritual development to be arrested. They stopped learning years ago and their conduct is that of a child. It's true that Jesus said the greatest thing in the world is the childlike spirit; but there is a tremendous difference between the childlike and the childish spirit. Peter Pan makes a charming play on the stage; but the man who will not grow up is a tragedy in real life. Let us passionately desire spiritual maturity and leave behind childish things!

Prophetically

We've all experienced heartbreaking events throughout our lives. To some these circumstances have become valuable lessons that have propelled them forward, while others have allowed the issues to negatively influence their spiritual walk. During the month of Tevet the Lord will impart great mercy to overcome those things that have been disruptive, if you'll allow it! Many of you believe that the Lord is in heaven devising your next test. In reality He stands ready to extend mercy so you can take the things that have been hurtful in the past and turn them into something you can build your future on. So during this month the Lord wants you to look to the future and see Him standing at the end of each situation, arms open wide, congratulating you on the victory!

It's the month to break the power of the evil watchers. Demonic surveillance is purposed to discover a way to take your blessings or steal your joy. You must, during this season, stick your finger in their eyes (pray) and not allow them to see the plans that the Lord has for you. You need to realize that satan and his minion's can only sabotage what you allow.

During Tevet you must pray for the leaders in your life. Satan knows that if he can remove your leaders he gains access to you. One way he can eliminate your oversight is to cause your soul to position itself against them, causing you to hold them in contempt (disrespect). Be careful to watch your attitude this month and walk it out circumspectly (cautiously). Pray for your leader and honor what the Lord is doing through them to bring you to a higher place in God's Kingdom. Furthermore, pray that the Lord seals them from any demonic attack purposed to take them out.

Tevet is the month of holy anger or righteous indignation. In other words be angry during this season about what satan is trying to do, but don't sin! Within your emotions there exists a fine line that when you cross it you pass over into areas that open the door to destruction. This month it's important that you deal with the issues that create anger in you or at specific times you'll erupt.

It is the month of return and redefinition, this is a good time to question whether you should ride through life as a passive traveler, looking out the window as you're driven to parts unknown, or whether to do something spiritually that will redirect or redefine you. Therefore, it's a good time to fast asking the Lord to extend great mercy. Remember passivity and lethargy never take risks and nothing godly can be built from it. During Tevet, to be the man or woman God has destined you to be, you should fast and earnestly pray; take steps of faith and leave behind those things that have imprisoned you!

Seek the Lord during this season about your next phase of life. It is like planting a seed. The seed sits in the ground, with no apparent results until the spring, when it germinates. Just because you can't see it doesn't mean that nothing is taking place. It means that whatever occurs, is happening underground away from our eyes. Look for the Lord, during Tevet, to begin a new work in you.

The tribe of Dan was one of the last in the procession as the Israelites journeyed through the desert. They were tasked with picking up the lost articles, which the other tribes had left behind as they traveled, and then they returned them to the people. Therefore, during Tevet the Lord will return lost things that have been stolen, misplaced or lost. Prophesy that there will be lost money found, bills canceled and paid off, commissions and bonuses awarded, favor on the job and blessings released!

The letter of Tevet is "eyin," literally meaning eye, which is ironic because this is the month when nothing is seen. It takes discernment to detect the hidden spiritual developments of this month. Discernment along with wisdom creates a place where the Creator can reveal His plan for you. So during this season ask the Lord to increase your discernment and wisdom.

The Bible compares people to trees, saying that man is like a tree of the field. Like the tree we are composed of roots, a trunk with branches and leaves along with fruit. So man is comprised of three aspects. The most important is our faith, like the root of the tree, faith is hidden, yet it's the underlying foundation. If your roots are strong, all the wind in the world won't uproot you. When ones faith is strong one doesn't waver in commitment. So during this month ask the Lord for increased faith.

The liver is the organ that's linked with this month. It's the center of your metabolism, a complex chemical factory and filter that controls the body's absorption of food. It carries out more than 500 separate processes concerned with regulating all the main chemicals in the blood (it purifies the blood) and many other life-supporting functions. The similarity between the liver and our Christian experience is that they can be both life giving. In the case of the liver, what you put into your body affects it causing life or destruction. It's the same principle in the spiritual dimension; you get out of it what you invest in it. So during Tevet, ask for those things that will not only enhance your spiritual maturity but also cause you to eat the solid food of the Spirit!

During the month of Tevet your testimony will reveal your

immaturity or maturity. Did what cause you to compromise your standard last year, do the same thing this year? Did you get offended this year just as you did last year? If so you may be stuck in a cycle of being spiritually underdeveloped! Only the Lord can help <u>you</u> rework your attitude. You must choose to allow Him to do whatever is necessary to change your disposition. This month you must be focused not only on what the Lord is delivering you from but also the direction He is leading you. Be careful not to get ahead of Him or lag too far behind, you must stay in step with the Holy Spirit! Now is the season to declare to the Lord to open "The Gate of Spiritual Maturity!"

The Gate of Spiritual Maturity
Prophetic Declarations

<u>Declare prophetically over your life, church, and the seven spheres of influence that</u>:

- The Gate of Spiritual Maturity is opened.
- Mercy from the Lord is released to build the future.
- The power of the evil watchers is broken and they cannot see the future plans the Lord has in store.
- A right attitude concerning leaders is exhibited through honor and prayer sealing them from any demonic attack.
- Righteous indignation arises toward the enemy.
- Steps of faith are taken leaving behind everything that is a hindrance.
- Jesus is beginning a new work internally.
- The Lord is returning lost things that have been stolen, lost money found, bills canceled and paid off, commissions and bonuses awarded; favor on the job and blessings released.
- The Lord is increasing wisdom and discernment.
- Increased faith is causing a more committed walk with the Lord.
- The Holy Spirit is leading and we are not getting ahead or lingering too far behind.

"In order to transform our environment we <u>must</u> change."

Scripture References

Hebrews 5:11-14
I Peter 2:2
I Corinthians 2:6, 3:2, 14:20
Ephesians 4:13

Prayer Proclamations

<u>Hebrews 5:13-14</u> "Anyone who lives on milk, being still an infant, is not acquainted with the teaching about righteousness. But solid food is for the mature, <u>who by constant use</u> have trained themselves to distinguish good from evil."

****

<u>PRAY THAT</u>:
- We ask the Lord to transform our hearts
- We value the spiritual wealth we have been blessed to receive (Luke 10:42)
- We are willing to pay the price (Matthew 10:38; Philippians 3:8)
- The Lord will give us a burden to pray for those in leadership (James 5:16)
- We passionately seek our spiritual identity (II Timothy 1:12; Ephesians 4:20-24)
- We follow the Holy Spirit's direction in fasting and prayer (Joel 2:12; Matthew 6:17-18)
- We have increased spiritual eyesight/discernment (I Corinthians 2:6-16)
- We are faithful to share our testimony (Acts 5:20, 18:9, 22:15)
- We are people of perseverance (James 1:2-4)

<u>REPENT and REFUSE TO PARTNER WITH</u>:
- Focus on earthly desires and passions
- Worldly anger, rage, malice
- Wanting the easy road
- Accusation

- Rebellion
- Familiarity/Lack of respect for leadership
- Spiritual blindness
- Fear/Ashamed to testify about Jesus

****

***<u>James 1:2</u>** "Consider it pure joy, my brothers, whenever you face trials of many kinds, because you know that the testing of your faith develops perseverance. Perseverance must finish its work so that you may be mature and complete, not lacking anything."*

Chapter Sixteen

The Gate of Fruitfulness

"And we pray this is order that you may live a life worthy of the Lord and may please him in every way; bearing fruit in every good work, growing in the knowledge of God."
~ *Colossians 1:10*

Overview

According to Hebraic custom the eleventh month (Zechariah 1:7) on the Jewish calendar is "Shevat" and it begins in January and ends in February on the Gregorian calendar. The tribe associated with this month is "Asher" and it means "pleasure, happiness, delicious and fatness," it's also Rosh Hashanah (New Years) for Trees. The gate name is "The Gate of Fruitfulness."

General Information

In Webster's dictionary "fruitful" defined is producing fruit conducive for a plentiful yield, and being abundantly productive. Among the number of Hebrew words for fruit or fruit producing, I would like to focus on the word "Karpophoreo," which means to bear fruit, crops, or figuratively to bear fruit in the heart (Luke 8:9-15). The Lord created Adam and Eve (Genesis 1:26), endowing them with moral, intellectual and spiritual power (Ephesians 4:24; Colossians 3:10) and He said to them, "Be <u>fruitful</u> and increase in number; fill the earth and subdue it" (to conquer and bring into subjection) (Genesis 1:28). This implies that Adam and Eve's offspring (you and I) were not only to be their physical fruit but also to be endowed with <u>moral</u>, <u>intellectual</u> and <u>spiritual power</u>, since we too, were made in "the image of God" (Genesis 1:27, 9:6; II Corinthians 4:4). Shevat is a month when the Jews celebrate "Rosh Hashanah (the New Year) for Trees." Man has been compared in the scriptures to trees, as it relates to growth and the yielding of fruit. For instance, a tree is created from a seed; it grows from the nutrition that it receives from the sun, soil and its root system. It then bears fruit and from its seed reproduces a tree of its kind which is the growth and fruit-producing pattern of man. From a biblical perspective there are numerous references to fruit and spiritual growth. For instance, "the fruit of your labor" is found in Psalm 128:2; activities of the godly are called "the fruit of the righteous" in Proverbs 11:30 and those who reject God's wisdom are described as eating "the fruit of their ways… filled with the fruit of their schemes" found in Proverbs 1:31 and Jeremiah 6:19. "The fruit of the lips," the blessings of one's speech, adds blessings to one's daily life found in Proverbs 12:14, 13:2, 18:20-21. Jesus and John the Baptist taught that the disciple is to produce fruit (good works) as evidence of true repentance, Matthew 3:8 and Luke 13:2-3 also explained that good trees (the repentant person) cannot produce bad fruit. On the other hand, a life filled with wicked acts, creating a bad tree (an unrepentant person) cannot produce good fruit, that is, a life of godly works (Matthew 3:10, 7:16-20; Luke 3:9, 6:43).

The Gate of Fruitfulness

To aid Christians in their walk before the Lord, God-given wisdom is made available, whose "fruit is better than fine gold" (Proverbs 8:19). The Holy Spirit develops within the Christian the fruit of "love, joy, peace, patience, kindness, goodness, faithfulness, gentleness, and self-control" (Galatians 5:2-23). To make the spiritual point that God's disobedient people need His mercy and saving power to heal them; Jeremiah refers to the healing affect of the balm or gum oil of a well-known bush/small tree growing in Gilead (Jeremiah 8:22, 46:11). From this comes the healing balm of Gilead, which means "a balm for spiritual healing." Thus, with the enablement of the Holy Spirit, the Christian can flourish "like a tree planted by streams of living waters, which yield its fruit in season" (Psalm 1:3). This analogy will be extremely important as you pray that the Lord open "The Gate of Fruitfulness."

PROPHETICALLY

During the time of Shevat it will be important to decide whether you're going to produce spiritual fruit for the future or not. As a blossom produces its aroma, this is a sign that fruit is about to appear. So during this season examine if you're blossoming, and if you are, then expect your life to bear fruit.

This month you should consider what the Lord is doing in your life in order to sustain your future generations. In other words, consider what He has imparted to you and begin the process of passing the riches of that knowledge down to those who are your offspring (children).

Jews classified Shevat as the month of "Tzadik," meaning "your righteousness becomes your foundation." Allow the Lord to assist you to become a person who has a righteous character, one who walks with holy standards. So surrender your time, and pursue His righteous kingdom, so that His principles can operate in your life. Also, during this season, you should inspect who is planted with you in your field (circle of influence) and ensure that they're also producing fruit. It's a time for you to connect and relate with the people who are trees in your life, meaning your family, friends, employer and spiritual authority, developing a new level of relationship with them. If fruit is lacking in these relationships do your part to assist those who don't have spiritual outgrowth to become fruitful.

In the plant kingdom water is a part of sustaining life that saturates the root system of the plant. It's during Shevat that the roots of your spiritual life will be awakened to the water of life (the Lord). So be aware that the river of God is forging its way to sustain you, so during Shevat shout, "My blessings are on the way!" because the water from God's throne is coming to satisfy the thirst of your root system.

During Shevat you need to dig for a greater purpose in every basic spiritual activity you do, you should never have, "just another day at church, at home or at your place of employment." By allowing the Word of God (Bible) to saturate your life and by surrendering to the guidance of the Holy Spirit, you will discover ways to glean the fruit of intimacy with the Lord, opening the way for you to eat of the sweet and succulent fruit of God's Kingdom. As long as you don't leave your heart untilled, or don't accept life as it comes, but make an effort to pick from the tree of God's provision, you will reap great treasures in His Kingdom. So allow the Lord to help you harvest those things that He has permitted you to gather during Shevat.

One observance of the 15th of Shevat teaches us that your service to the Lord should not remain limited to those matters, which are merely necessary, in other words, "I'll do just what's needed." Believers must constantly walk in passion as it applies to the things of God bringing pleasure to both the Creator and the believer. No matter how lofty a Christian's present level of anointing, he or she cannot remain static (lacking movement), but must always go higher. So during Shevat, ask the Lord to infuse you with fervor renouncing any lack of spiritual movement, action or change that's designed to separate you from the Lord.

Because the 15th of Shevat is celebrated in the Jewish community as "Rosh Hashanah for Trees" it's a time to give first fruit offerings. The Jew insured that the fruit tree bore wonderful and luscious fruit and gladly gave a portion of their harvest to the Lord in the form of a first fruit offering. So this month discern where the Lord has blessed you and cheerfully give Him your first fruits.

In Jewish tradition, the entire book of Deuteronomy was Moses' last speech, and he gave it over the last five weeks of his life. Custom submits that he started on the first of Shevat and that the average person who was there listening to him began to feel spiritual growth on the 15th of Shevat. Therefore, this month is an important time for spiritual growth because its growth and longevity coupled with pruning and meticulous care that causes the fruit of a tree to be sweet and rich. So permit the Lord to influence your life allowing the growth that comes from Him to become obvious.

The sense of this month is eating and tasting, such as "...Taste and see that the Lord is good..." (Psalm 34:8). Eating requires grinding and pulverizing your food for proper digestion. This month you must chew on the goodness of the Lord allowing His principles to settle in your heart so that it can become beneficial to your spiritual growth. You should understand that chewing opens the inner flavor of food. This bursting of flavor, during Shevat, speaks to the spiritual savor of the Lord's gift of revelation that has been given to you. So this month allow the fullness of what the Lord is releasing to completely saturate your life and radically change you forevermore.

Just as the earth conceals the greatest treasures beneath the surface both in the form of precious metals and gems, as well as in the productive energies locked in the soil; so it is with each of us. The capacity to discover huge reserves of godly wealth has been placed in you. You simply need to ask the Holy Spirit to help you this month, mine the spiritual treasures hidden beneath your surface that the Lord has imparted, and allow Him to "dig up the earth (heart)" so that you may glean the blessings of His abundance. Also you should plant seeds in His soil and watch them take root, blossom, bear fruit and multiply for the future. So cry out to the Lord to reveal the riches that He has given and anticipate your harvest in God's Kingdom.

Even as the woman was at the well and she gave Jesus water to drink (John 4: 1-26), you must look for those who are bringing pitchers of water to you. Moreover, be careful that you don't make wrong decisions because you think that you are not being properly watered. Even as the woman at the well felt divided because of her prejudices and wrong mindsets the

Lord revealed to her who He was and brought great revelation and peace to her. Even so watch carefully who gives you water because it may be the Lord and you may be dismissing Him as someone other than who He is! Look for a greater level of interaction with the Holy Spirit and watch for living waters to be supplied in unusual ways. Just find your way to the well and receive from Him the depth of His cool enriching waters.

Colossians 1:10 says, "And we pray this in order that you may live a life worthy of the Lord and may please him in every way, bearing fruit in every good work, growing in the knowledge of God." During Shevat we need to ask the Lord to flourish in our hearts, homes, church and city. It's vitally important that you spend quality time with the Lord asking Him to increase the fruitfulness in your life. One way that you'll know you're about to bear fruit is that you are blossoming!

This is the month that the Lord wants you to experience <u>fruitfulness</u> not <u>barrenness</u>, so petition the Lord to till up your ground, prune your branches and connect you to the source of life and watch your blossoms produce fruit!

** Because a Daniel fast involves eating fruit and vegetables this is a good season to fast. Please pray and ask the Lord what day or days He would have you fast this month. I would also recommend reading and studying the book of Daniel throughout Shevat. **

Gate of Fruitfulness
Prophetic Declarations

Declare prophetically over your life, church, and the seven spheres of influence that:

- The Gate of Fruitfulness is opened.
- Spiritually I am blossoming and bearing godly fruit.
- What the Lord has given will pass to my offspring.
- A righteous character and holy standard is developing.
- Those who are planted in my field (circle of influence) are producing fruit.
- Family, friends, employers and spiritual authorities are connecting and relating at a deeper level.
- The roots of spiritual life are satisfied by the Lord.
- The river of God sustains me, cry out, "My blessings are on the way!"
- The fruit of intimacy with the Lord brings life.
- God's provision and great treasures in His Kingdom manifest.
- Walking in spiritual passion brings pleasure to the Creator and myself.
- Cheerfully giving first fruit offerings releases the Lord's monetary blessings.

"In order to transform our environment we <u>must</u> change."

Scripture References

Genesis 1:26-28, 9:6

Jeremiah 6:19, 8:22, 46:11

Psalm 1:3, 128:2

Proverbs 1:31, 11:30, 12:14, 13:2, 18:20-21

Matthew 3:8-10, 7:16-20

Luke 3:9, 6:43-45, 8:9-15

John 15:1-8

Galatians 5:2-23

Ephesians 4:24

Colossians 3:10

II Corinthians 4:4

PRAYER PROCLAMATIONS

<u>Luke 6:44-45</u> *"<u>Each tree is recognized by its own fruit</u> …For out of the overflow of his heart his mouth speaks."*

<u>Galatians 5:9</u> *"For <u>the fruit of the light</u> consists in all goodness, righteousness and truth…"*

****

<u>PRAY THAT</u>:
- We ask the Lord to transform our hearts
- We are bearing good fruit for the kingdom (John 15:16)
- We are growing in the knowledge of God (Romans 5:3-4; II Peter 1:5-7)
- We are strengthened with God's might (John 15:4-5)
- We are growing in endurance (John 15:2)
- We are growing in patience (Galatians 5:22-23)
- We are joyfully giving thanks to the Father for our inheritance (Isaiah 35:10; John 16:24; Romans 14:17)
- We are recognized as belonging to Jesus by the righteous fruit of our lips (Philippians 1:11)

<u>REPENT and REFUSE TO PARTNER WITH</u>:
- Barrenness/Fruitlessness/Refusal to be pruned
- Dormant/Sluggish growth
- Baal - Receiving our significance/power from the world
- Childishness/Refusing to grow up
- Leviathan/Anti-Christ – Twisting the truth about God
- Complaining/Accusation/Ingratitude toward God or one another

- Fruits of the sinful nature: anger, sexual immorality, jealousy (Galatians 5:19-21)

****

<u>*Colossians 1:10*</u> *"...<u>in order that you may live a life worthy of the Lord and may please him in every way</u>: bearing fruit in every good work, growing in the knowledge of God, being strengthened with all power according to his glorious might, so that you may have great endurance and patience, and joyfully giving thanks to the Father, who has qualified you to share in the inheritance of the saints in the kingdom of light."*

Chapter Seventeen

The Gate of Joy

"When your words came, I ate them; they were my joy and my heart's delight, for I bear your name, O Lord God Almighty."
~ *Jeremiah 15:16*

OVERVIEW

According to Hebraic custom the <u>twelfth month</u> (Esther 3:7) on the Jewish calendar is "<u>Adar;</u>" it begins in February and ends in March on the Gregorian calendar. The tribe associated with this month is "<u>Naphtali</u>" and it means "<u>my struggle</u>" (Genesis 30:8). At the end of your struggle you will have joy! *The adage is, "When Adar comes, joy is increased,"* therefore, the gate name is "The Gate of <u>Joy</u>."

GENERAL INFORMATION

Joy is a feeling that comes from success, good fortune, or a sense of well being; it's a source of happiness. The question is, "How does one attain joy consistently?" Possibly the best spiritual explanation comes from using the word as an acronym. "J" represents Jesus, "Y" stands for "You," and the

"O" signifies "Zero," or nothing. Meaning, true lasting joy is found when "nothing" comes between "Jesus" and "You!"

Each of us must determine what type of joy we want. Do you desire joy that comes from spiritual success that's lasting, or from natural good fortune that's temporal? Spiritually, a sense of well being or happiness occurs through a process of adjustments, surrender, persistence, trust, alignment and more importantly, relationship with the Lord. Your decision to allow these elements to work in your life shifts you from one spiritual dimension to another producing an environment where the Lord can touch your circumstances, resulting in kingdom joy. Just settle in your heart that you're going the way of the Lord no matter the circumstances. David, for instance, rejoiced over God's righteousness (Psalm 71:14-16), His salvation (Psalm 21:1, 71:23), mercy (Psalm 31:7), creation (Psalm 148:5), word (Psalm 119:14, 162), faithfulness (Psalm 33:1-6), God's holy character, as well as His mighty acts, even in the midst of great turmoil. It was his selfless and steadfast understanding of God that enabled him to experience joy as evidenced through his writings in Psalms.

Far and above, happiness experienced through righteous people (Psalm 150; Philippians 4:4) is actually produced by the Holy Spirit (Galatians 5:22), this kind of joy looks beyond the present to your future godly solution (Romans 5:2, 8:18; I Peter 1:4,6). The Spirit of the Lord causes you to see the sovereignty of God, who works out all things for your ultimate good, even when your mind tells you to believe otherwise. This unspeakable joy is distinct from mere happiness, joy like this is possible, even in the midst of great turmoil (I Corinthians 12:26; II Corinthians 6:10, 7:4).

Prophetically

Adar is when the Jewish people celebrate Purim. During this time reflect on the book of Esther because it's the story of how Queen Esther and Mordechai saved the Jewish people from certain destruction. Purim is a holiday of light and gladness, joy and honor and it's closely associated with fasting. Fasting is accomplished in preparation for, or in memory of something. So celebrate what the Lord has done in your life through prayer and fasting. The Purim narrative is not a tale of ancient history, but instead it contains fundamental lessons relevant to us today. <u>First</u>, just like the Jewish people during the time of Esther, we have to realize that we (Christians) are in exile. Although our parents and grandparents may have lived where we live it's not our home. Our home is actually found in the kingdom of heaven and in the revelation of Jesus Christ. <u>Second</u>, even though we live here in the earthly realm, we have to guard ourselves against thinking like those who don't have the truth of Jesus. Remember you are just passing through this life in preparation for your eternal life. It's during Purim that you are reminded of your close relationship with Jesus and the kingdom that He is preparing for you. <u>Third</u>, miracles are possible at all times and in all situations. The Lord is not bound by the laws of nature and can bend nature at His bidding. Just because you haven't seen a miracle recently doesn't mean they don't exist. Allow your faith to increase, as you believe that "with God nothing is impossible." <u>Fourth</u>, God's miracles need not upset the natural order, but can manifest within them. Miracles don't have to necessarily happen around you, they can occur whenever the Lord deems it necessary, so they can materialize even in the midst of the darkest surroundings. So during this season, you must realize that your home is really not of this world, and you must guard yourself from becoming worldly. Moreover, you must believe that miracles can be experienced anytime the Lord desires and they can happen in any environment the Lord sees fit. He, many times, doesn't work according to your schedule but will accomplish the miracle at His good pleasure.

In reading the book of Esther pay particular attention to both the main characters of the Purim narrative, Mordechai and Esther. They did not sit in their positions of honor and try to save the people from afar. Instead they put their lives on the line, risking everything to change a situation. In other words they become <u>intentional</u>! The Lord's saying it's time to arise and lay everything on the line.

Why did the Jewish people set aside Adar as the month to be joyous? The answer is that the nation of Israel was saved from annihilation during this time. Haman sought to destroy the entire nation of Israel solely because of his hatred for one Jewish person, Mordechai. Since the entire Jewish population in the world at that time lived in the empire that was ruled by King Xerxes, the future of the Jewish people and Judaism was threatened. Mordechai does a gutsy thing by conveying to Queen Esther, a Jew (Esther 2:17) that she must go to the king, who is her husband, and plead for her people. Her actions teach us two timely lessons: 1) that there is no prayer and request like that of the community and 2) that God's intervention normally comes out of crisis.

Because the Jews prayed to the Lord in a spirit of unity (as one), God performed a miracle for them, Haman was killed, Mordechai was made the king's minister, Esther's life was spared and the Jews were saved. From this event joy became very apparent throughout the land, and "The Festival of Purim" was implemented. It was a time of overwhelming happiness when they further committed to the Lord and to the principles of the Torah (Bible). Because of this spiritual redemptive transformation the Jews celebrate throughout the entire month of Adar (as well as Adar II during leap year). Great joy comes to us when we realize that you and I can experience great transformation just as the Jewish people experienced during the reign of Esther.

During this month it's important to know that you have a spiritual identity and mission in God's Kingdom. Some of us never tap into our identity in the supernatural dimension we just try to be totally natural. We must remove the masquerade (false identity) and enter into our true identity with laughter. Ask the Lord, during Adar, "What is my spiritual identity and how do I walk in it?" Demons recognize your heavenly signature because it's written on you. Because they (demons) can see it, you might as well become it! So ask the Lord to define who you are in the Spirit and help you accomplish what He's deposited in you! Many of you don't know your spiritual identity because you've not inquired of Him and others have resisted their spiritual identity because it's easier to trust themselves more than the Lord. It's time to leave behind the fear that's driven you and become intentional for the Lord's purposes. What Mordechai and Esther did for Israel is much like what occurs in the physical body when a virus invades it. It first infects the host and then those around it. Allow the Lord to intentionally infect you with the virus of His Kingdom and watch how it spreads to those around you!

Adar is the time when Jesus told His disciples to find the coin in the mouth of the fish. So during this month allow the hidden things of the kingdom to become the source of your blessings. When the enemy tells you that you cannot succeed, declare during Adar, that the Lord has defined you and the riches of His Kingdom, and not the world system, is your portion. Profess that nothing will move you from the Lord's presence and that the precious Blood of Jesus protects you!

It's during Adar that you are to renounce anxiety and declare that the supply line of God's Kingdom be released to you. If you'll refute anxiety you'll see provision the Lord has for you. With the help of the Holy Spirit conquer your fear and allow the Lord to shower down His promises upon you. Moreover, it's the month of laughter abounding in joy. It's a time of witnessing life impact darkness with the light of God's Glory. It's the time when the power of barrenness is broken in your life. Meaning whatever darkness is encroaching upon you laugh at it and watch God permeate it. It's the time that God has ordained that your fear "shall laugh." Because this is the month of the spleen, the root of depression and despair must break so faith can come forth in your thought process. During Adar the Lord wants to pull out the root of depression and despair declaring that it will not affect you anymore! These two bondages are passion killers so don't partner at any level with what the enemy wants to do through them!

It's worth noting that in all cases, where the tribes of Israel and their heads are mentioned, the tribe of Naphtali is mentioned last. There is an old rabbinic adage that says, "The last is often the most favored." It is important to know that Naphtali followed the tribe of Dan collecting things that the tribe of Dan left behind as they journeyed through the desert. So expect the favor of the Lord to come upon you and decree that lost things are returned and items that were stolen are recovered or replaced!

Adar is the time that Moses was born and because he was the deliverer of Israel this month your deliverance is forming round about you to usher in transformation. Where you have given up hope for major breakthroughs in your life you need to allow the Lord to shatter ungodly mindsets, unholy principles, or ungodly alliances that hold you captive. It's also the time where ungodly decrees are going to be broken over you, so allow the Holy Spirit to reveal those things that have negatively affected you.

This is the month to develop your war strategy against the anti-Christ spirit. Remember the anti-Christ spirit represents any situation where Jesus is not central in your life, so don't let the giants produce fear in you causing you not to move forward; guard yourself from idolatry.

The Lord desires to interact with you like never before. He wants to remove those things that have separated you from Him. Perhaps you feel the Lord is angry with you, maybe you're angry with Him, or you feel He's abandoned you.

Let this month be the time that you allow Him to touch your heart and fill you with the joy of His presence, which is the scaffold that helps repair the breach between you and Him. So be happy during Adar for He desires relationship with you!

The Lord is dealing with your enemies suddenly this month and causing great increase to come to you. Psalm 18:28-29 says, "You, O Lord, keep my lamp burning; my God turns my darkness into light. With your help I can advance against a troop, with my God I can scale a wall." Through faith and dependency upon the Lord there is nothing that can stand against you so take a big leap in the Lord.

Declare that the Lord is delivering you from any deep hidden issues or bondages (ungodly beliefs) that mask the real you. This is the season to decree healing in your life. Allow faith to arise and speak to your circumstances seeing your infirmities, physically and emotionally, dissolve. Begin to command that miraculous signs and wonders break out in your life causing increased faith and then celebrate!

Another interpretation of Naphtali is "a deer let loose." The blessing of Naphtali is included in the concept of being swift and having the ability to harvest quickly. So during this season expect to be given abilities by God to glean rapidly. One of the best verses to shout out loud this month is "The Lord will make my feet like hinds' feet" (Habakkuk 3:19). You must declare that your harvest will increase and that you will become strong and agile to gather everything that the Lord has declared for you!

Don't allow the enemy's plan to take your inheritance this

year and watch for legal entrapments. If the enemy comes at you like a flood – the Lord will raise up a standard on your behalf! Develop a watch and prayer strategy around you. Jump up the wall that has been resisting you! Throw down those spirits that are hindering you and declare yourself free in Jesus Name!

This is the month to achieve an overall disconnect from the spirit of fear. Think for a moment about Esther, she moved past all her fears and stood with confidence before the king in order to overthrow her enemies. From this time forward let your communication be filled with faith. Allow your joy to be expressed through laughter as you move in new beginnings of trust. During Adar stand firm against depression and despair allowing faith thoughts to enter your inner-man and function in confidence trusting the Lord with all your heart and strength!

It's important you become change agents for Christ. The Lord wants your old religious mindsets to fall away and those things that have held you captive to disappear. He wants you to see His Kingdom as a powerful force in the earth today and not a powerless, religious system. You were not placed on this earth to meander but to be intentional and viral concerning the purposes of God.

Revelation 11:15 says; "...*The kingdom of the world has become the kingdom of our Lord and his Christ, and he will reign forever and ever.*" Because we are children of the King, you and I are to rule and reign just as our Father does. So during this season arise to fulfill your spiritual identity and celebrate!

It is important that during Adar you recognize what the Lord is doing, look for the small things that seem insignificant. Remember Adar is considered to be a wonderful time of great transformation, so celebrate what God has done and is doing in your life. Set aside time to rejoice choosing happiness as you pass through, "The Gate of Joy."

The Gate of Joy
Prophetic Declarations

<u>Declare prophetically over your life, church, and the seven spheres of influence that</u>:

- The Gate of Joy is opened.
- Nothing comes between Jesus and me.
- The Lord is doing great things!
- Spiritual identity reveals your mission in God's Kingdom.
- The hidden things of God's Kingdom are the source of blessings.
- The supply line of God's Kingdom is being released.
- The light of God's Glory is dispelling darkness.
- The root of depression and despair is pulled out so that faith can arise.
- Things that have been stolen by the enemy are recovered.
- Deliverance is forming around me allowing the Lord to shatter ungodly mindsets, principles or alliances that hold me captive.
- Jesus is the Savior who destroys the works of the anti-Christ spirit.
- The Lord is filling me with the joy of His presence.

"In order to transform our environment we <u>must</u> change."

PRAYER PROCLAMATIONS

<u>*Jeremiah 15:16*</u> *"When your words came, I ate them; they were my joy and my heart's delight, for I bear your name, O Lord God Almighty."*

****

<u>PRAY THAT</u>:
- We ask the Lord to transform our hearts
- We know our spiritual identity – "Who am I created to be?" (Psalm 139:13-16; Jeremiah 1:5)
- We are obedient to God's vision/plan for us - (Judges 6:14; I Kings 19:19; Isaiah 6:8; Acts 26:16)
- We are in relationship and submission to one another (Esther 4:15-17, 8:11, 9:2, 15-17)
- We believe God wants to grant abundance (Psalm 84:11)
- We can laugh at earthly circumstances (Esther 9:23-28; Proverbs 31:25)
- We know that God loves us, even in our weakness (John 18:27, 21:15-19)

<u>REPENT and REFUSE TO PARTNER WITH</u>:
- Worldly identities or alliances
- Rebellion against spiritual authority
- Depression and despair
- Anxiety and stress
- Doubt and fear
- Oppression
- Anti-Christ spirit

****

Esther 9:1 *"On the thirteenth day of the twelfth month, the month of Adar, the edict commanded by the king was to be carried out. On this day the enemies of the Jews had hoped to overpower them, <u>but now the tables were turned and the Jews got the upper hand over those who hated them</u>."*

Psalm 30:11-12 *"You turned my wailing into dancing; you removed my sackcloth and clothed me with joy ... O Lord my God, I will give you thanks forever."*

Chapter Eighteen

The Gate of Transformation

"Do not conform any longer to the pattern of this world, but be transformed by the renewing of your mind. Then you will be able to test and approve what God's will is – his good, pleasing and perfect will."
~ Romans 12:2

OVERVIEW

According to Hebraic custom the thirteenth month on the Jewish calendar is "Adar II" and it begins in February and ends in March on the Gregorian calendar. A year with 13 months is referred to in Hebrew as a pregnant year. February 29, the extra day added to the Gregorian calendar is commonly known as our leap year. The additional month is known as Adar I, Adar Alef (first Adar). The extra month is inserted before the regular month of Adar known in such years as Adar II. Note that Adar II is the "real" Adar, the one in which Purim is celebrated each year. Adar I is the "extra" month. The tribe associated with this month is "Levi" and it means "joined or unity." According to Genesis 29:31-34, Leah said when she gave birth to Levi, "Now my husband will be joined with me,"

Leah's life was <u>transformed</u> from sadness to joy because she assumed that Jacob would now love and be devoted to her as a result of the third son that she gave him. The gate name is "The Gate of <u>Transformation</u>."

General Information

The word transformation means to change in form, appearance, or structure; to metamorphose. Biblically, transformation means to change radically in inner character, condition, or nature. In Romans 12:2 the Apostle Paul exhorted Christians, "Do not be conformed to this world, but be transformed by the renewing of your mind." Followers of Christ should not be conformed, either inwardly or in appearance, to the values, ideals, and behavior of this fallen world. Believers should continually renew their minds through prayer and the study of God's Word, by the power of the Holy Spirit, and so be transformed and made like Christ (II Corinthians 3:18). Further instances of transformation occur when the Lord returns for us, He will "transform our lowly bodies that it may be conformed to His glorious body" (Philippians 3:21).

Under general practice of living and following the Holy Spirit, we discover and develop our strength to glorify God. We also, when guided by the Holy Spirit, dig back into our past to face our hurts and acquire needed healing.

After salvation, we began the journey of growth and transformation becoming more like Christ (Romans 8:29), not having confidence on our own ability but on the new identity of Christ within (Colossians 1:27; II Corinthians 4:7). As new believers, our simple child-like faith compelled us to act according to His will and good purpose (Philippians 2:12-13). The question is, "Have we abandoned this way of life and opted for a lifestyle that is superficial and mundane?"

The process of transformation is designed to bring us into the fullness of Christ. Apostle Paul said it this way, "Let this mind be in you which is Christ Jesus." The aim of the believer is to have the "mind of Christ," so we might see all things in order to evaluate all things, to respond to our surroundings the way Jesus would.

My hope is that you have truly been transformed into Jesus' likeness. Religious activity or living our Christian experience through works of the flesh or performance will cause great disappointment. True transformation occurs when we are filled with the peace, joy and power of the Lord, which reflects His majesty in our lives.

PROPHETICALLY

Adar II is a month where great change will transpire, so choose to be receptive as the Lord transforms issues in your life. Personally, this month expect the Lord to end certain seasons that are non-productive for His Kingdom, meaning we need to celebrate the end of a matter and the beginning of something new. Spiritually, our happiness is established on the truth that the Lord has performed a miracle or He is in the process of accomplishing one! No matter where you are in the Christian journey, shout with joy declaring that this is the time for new beginnings!

In order to unify believers and create a long lasting change, each of us like Esther, must begin to assume a more aggressive spiritual role. Esther, prior to her encounter with the king, took responsibility by instructing Mordechai to assemble the people to fast and pray about Israel's potential demise. It is from this example of the nation of Israel humbling itself, asking God for direction, that we must derive a valuable lesson. We must first humble ourselves before the Lord and then ask for His guidance. Each of us has been commissioned by the Lord to carry out His requests without delay! So this is the time to see what the enemy is doing and rise up in victory, which was won for us through Christ's suffering and death on the cross, declaring that satan can no longer ensnare us through accusation, independence and self-focus.

All of the phenomena of Adar and Purim are essentially represented states of transformation. The method in the Torah, which models this phenomenon, is the wisdom of permutation or of complete transformation. It was the faith and action of Esther and Mordechai that turned an otherwise bleak situation into liberation for the nation of Israel. During this month cry out, just as Esther did for God's justice to arise, and, by faith, the Lord will completely transform your circumstances.

"Kuf" is the prevailing word that is used during Adar II. The Hebraic translation means "the eye of a needle." From a revelatory perspective, a glorious breakthrough happens when we endure being pulled through the eye of the needle. Instead of reacting in frustration and abandoning the process (deliverance) because circumstances have become more difficult, consider this to be the vehicle that will shift you to the next spiritual level. Just as a seed that is planted in the ground, at first is buried and unseen, does it mean that nothing is happening? Time will ultimately reveal that the seed was in a process of development. Even so the true identity of what the Lord is accomplishing in our life is many times obscure to the natural eye, and we must allow Him to reveal the fruit of His labor at His good pleasure not ours. Therefore, this is the month to permit the outgrowth in your life to come to a higher realm. Trust the Lord to metamorphose your inner man into a useable vessel for Him. Don't become angry because you are in an unfamiliar place and feel uncomfortable instead rely upon the Lord and believe He has begun a good work in you and will complete it (Philippians 1:6).

During Adar II be careful about worry because worry is inconsequential to God's Kingdom (Matthew 6:25-34). The Lord desires us to focus on what He wants fulfilled in our lives not the natural aspects of the world around us. Cast your cares upon the Lord and pray intently for His will, in other words it is the time to transform our worry into unspeakable joy!

Because the sense of the tribe of Levi is singing, due to the Levites service in the Temple, we should change our expression about issues that appear negative and sing over them. It is as we condition ourselves to stand in faith, praising the Lord in song, that He will recognize the signature of faith in us. Remember it is faith that pleases the Lord, so as we sing to our issues we release utterances of faith into God's Kingdom, in other words when we sing to our issues the Lord moves on our behalf.

When the Israelites left Egypt, the ancient manner of worship was still observed by them, the eldest son of each house inherited the priest's office. At Sinai the first change in the ancient practice was made. A hereditary priesthood in the family of Aaron was instituted (Exodus 28:1). But it was not until that terrible sin that occurred when the children of Israel worshipped the Golden Calf that the tribe of Levi stood apart and began to occupy a distinct position among the tribes of Israel (Exodus 32). The state of being the firstborn child was then conferred on this tribe, which henceforth was devoted to the service of the sanctuary (Numbers 3:11ff). They were selected for this purpose because of their zeal for the glory of God (Exodus 32:26), and because, as the tribe to which Moses and Aaron belonged, they would naturally stand by the lawgiver in his work. During this month let it be said of us that we have a zeal for the glory of the Lord and for those the Lord has placed over us. That each of us must bow our knees to the Lord denying the cult of self! We have been directed by I Peter 2:9, "But you are a chosen people, <u>a royal priesthood</u>, a holy nation, <u>a people belonging to God</u>, that you may declare the praises of him who called you out of darkness into his wonderful light." Since we are priests in God's Kingdom we should live a holy life separated unto the Lord. So this is the month to petition the Lord for the zeal and passion of the Levites.

The tribe of Levi was not included among the armies of Israel (Numbers 1:47, 2:33, 26:62), because they were reckoned to themselves. They were the special guardians of the tabernacle (Numbers 1:51, 18:22ff). The Gershonites pitched their tents on the west of the tabernacle (Numbers 3:23), the Kohathities on the south (Numbers 3:29), the Merarites on the north (Numbers 3:35), and the priests on the east (Numbers 3:38). It was their duty to move the tent and carry the parts of the sacred structure from place to place. They were given to Aaron and his sons, the priests, to wait upon them and do work for them at the sanctuary service (Numbers 8:19, 18:2ff). Where are you positioned to accomplish His work? You must vigilantly guard your assignment especially during Adar II. Allow the Holy Spirit to reveal where you are to serve and then do it with all of your heart! Stay in right alignment with His Spirit and He will guide you in all of His ways!

Because the tribe of Levi was wholly (completely) consecrated to the service of the Lord, they had no territorial possessions, God was their inheritance (Numbers 18:20, 26:62; Deuteronomy 18:1ff), and for their support it was ordained that they should receive from the other tribes of the produce of the land. Forty-eight cities also were assigned to them, thirteen of which were for the priests "to dwell in" along with their own inhabitants. Along with their dwellings they had "suburbs" or "commons" for their herds and flocks, and also fields and vineyards (Numbers 35:2ff).

Nine of these cities were in Judah, three in Naphtali, and four in each of the other tribes (Joshua 21). Six of the Levitical cities were set apart as "Cities of Refuge." Thus the Levites were scattered among the tribes to keep alive among them the knowledge and service of God. So during this month, allow the glory and presence of the Lord to touch and transform those around us. Declare that in times of financial pressure and lack that you are in God's economy not the world's. Each of us must recognize that prosperity is from our Father and every blessing we experience is because of His infinite love, grace and mercy. There is an overused cliché that goes something like this, "You can't out give the Lord." No matter the many times we have heard this statement, once we receive a revelation of its meaning our giving and lives will be transformed.

So during Adar II recognize what the Lord is doing, look for the small things that seem insignificant. Remember this month is advantageous for great transformation, so celebrate what God is doing in your life! Set aside time to rejoice choosing happiness as you pass through, "The Gate of Transformation."

The Gate of Transformation
PROPHETIC DECLARATIONS

<u>*Declare prophetically over your life, church, and the seven spheres of influence that*</u>:

- The Gate of Transformation is opened.
- The Lord transforms issues in lives.
- The season that is non-productive for the kingdom has ended.
- It is a time for new beginnings so shout for joy!
- Believers will assume a more aggressive spiritual role.
- Satan cannot ensnare through accusation, independence and self-focus.
- God's justice is arising.
- The inner man is metamorphosing to become a useable vessel for God.
- The work that the Lord has begun, He will complete.
- Worry is inconsequential to God's Kingdom.
- Worry is transforming into unspeakable joy!
- When we sing to our issues it releases faith utterances into the kingdom.
- Zeal and passion for the glory of the Lord is released.
- The cult of self is denied.
- Lives are holy and separated unto the Lord.

- The Lord is transforming those around us with His Glory and presence.
- Believers live according to God's economy not the world's.
- It is a time of celebration and rejoicing as we choose to be transformed.

"In order to transform our environment we <u>must</u> change."

The Gate of Transformation

PRAYER PROCLAMATIONS

<u>II Corinthians 3:18</u> *"...And we, who with unveiled faces all reflect the Lord's Glory, are being transformed into his likeness with ever-increasing glory, which comes from the Lord, who is the Spirit."*

****

<u>PRAY THAT</u>:
- We are transformed by the renewing of our minds (II Corinthians 3:18; Romans 8:29, 12:2)
- We pursue intimacy with the Lord through prayer and study of the Word (Song of Songs 1:1-4, 2:14; Psalm 27:4; Revelation 3:20)
- We yield to the Holy Spirit's guidance receiving healing from past hurts (Exodus 15:26; Hosea 6:1; Hebrews 12:1-13)
- We embrace radical change of our inner character (Philippians 3:21; I Corinthians 15:52-27)
- We are filled with the peace, joy and power of the Lord (John 20:21; Romans 14:17; 1 Peter 1:8; Galatians 1:3; 5:22)
- We are in alignment with God's timing for such a time as this (Esther 4:12-17)
- We humble ourselves before the Lord and clearly hear His direction (James 1:22-25; Philippians 2:12-13)
- We advance with increased faith in our hearts (Colossians 3:1-2; James 1:6)
- We release a new song to the Lord that will shatter the plans of the enemy (Psalm 33:3, 40:3, 144:9; 1 Peter 2:9)
- We have a zeal for the glory of the Lord (Exodus 33:18; II Corinthians 3:7-9)

REPENT and REFUSE TO PARTNER WITH:
- Conformity to this world
- Status quo — resistance to transformation
- Lack of passion
- Fear of change
- Independence and self-focus
- Performance and religious activity
- Control and manipulation

****

I Peter 2:9 *"...But you are a chosen people, a royal priesthood, a holy nation, a people belonging to God, that you may declare the praises of him who called you out of darkness into his wonderful light."*

Epilogue

From my heart to yours…

I hope what you have learned from *Victory at the Gates*, is that we need to be transformed! While the word transformation is currently a much-used buzzword, still many do not have a clear understanding of its meaning. To be transformed is to have a marked change in nature, form or appearance. True transformation occurs when we do not follow a formula but experience a genuine metamorphosis, just as a caterpillar evolves into a butterfly. From a Christian perspective, it is simply a choice. We must choose between our desire for worldly pleasure or the process that will begin our spiritual journey, toward the development of the character and nature of Jesus in us. Dear one, there are no short cuts! Without an authentic relationship with our Savior, we will never rule the gates of our cities without first allowing the Lord to rule the gates of our hearts.

The historical and prophetic information that I have shared is meant to support and enhance your passage from affection to an intimate, abiding relationship with the Lord. I must be clear, that neither religiosity nor performance is a substitute for your love affair with Him. Our Lord is our only hope for the future and our spiritual identity is only in Him. Once we allow the Lord to captivate our hearts we will begin to govern on earth as it is in heaven. We must see, through faith, God's Kingdom manifesting on earth. So, I beseech you to stand in the gap for this generation as we pave the way for, *"Victory at the Gates!"*

~

Matthew 7:7

"Ask and it will be given to you; seek and you will find; knock and the door will be opened to you. For anyone who asks receives; he who seeks finds; and to him who knocks, the door will be opened."

Matthew 6:10

"Your kingdom come, your will be done on earth as it is in heaven."

~

Matthew 22:37-40

"Jesus replied: "Love the Lord your God with all your heart and with all your soul and with all your mind. This is the first and greatest commandment. And the second is like it: 'Love your neighbor as yourself.' All the Law and the Prophets hang on these two commandments."

~

Romans 12:2

"Do not conform any longer to the pattern of this world, but be transformed by the renewing of your mind. Then you will be able to test and approve what God's will is – his good, pleasing and perfect will."

~

I Peter 1:14-15

"As obedient children, do not conform to the evil desires you had when you lived in ignorance. But just as he who called you is holy, so be holy in all you do; for it is written: "Be holy, because I am holy."

~

Revelation 11:15b

"…The kingdom of this world has become the kingdom of our Lord and of his Christ, and he will reign for ever and ever."

References

- Hamon, Dr. Bill (1991) Manual on Ministering Spiritual Gifts, "God's Prophetic Purpose for Praise." Chapter Five - page 25-26 of "Victory at the Gates."

- Thomas S. Rainer (1997) "The Bridger Generation." Chapter One - page 6 of "Victory at the Gates."

- George Barna, "Absolute Confusion." Chapter One - page 8 of "Victory at the Gates."

- Frank Gaebelein, "The Expositors Bible Commentary," referencing Genesis 1:26. Chapter One – page 11 of "Victory at the Gates."

- Elwell, A. Walter (2001) Baker Theological Dictionary of the Bible

- Morgan, J. Robert, Pierce, Chuck (2000) Stories, Illustrations & Quotes

- Pierce, Dr. Chuck (2006) Positioned for War Understanding the Significance of your Tribe [DVD 1] sessions 3 & 4 [DVD 2] sessions 5 & 6 -The Issachar School. Pierce, Dr. Chuck, Heidler, Dr. Robert (2006) Understand the Months Prophetically [DVD 2] sessions 3 & 4 [DVD 3] sessions 5 & 6 - The Issachar School. Pages 25, 27, 30-38, 41-46, 48, 49, 51, 53, 54, 55, 59, 60, 62, 63, 66, 67, 68, 76, 79-82.

- Holman, (1991) Holman Bible Dictionary defining "Revelation." Chapter Six – page 32 of "Victory at the Gates." Defining "Wealth." Chapter Seven – page 39 of

"Victory at the Gates."

- Davis, D. John (1972) Davis Dictionary of the Bible fourth revised addition.

- Barna, George (1998) the Second Coming of the Church – Chapter One – page 9 of "Victory at the Gates."

- Youngblood, R. F. (1995) New Illustrated Bible Dictionary. Chapter Two – page 10 of "Victory at the Gates." Defining "Righteousness." Chapter Seven – page 45 of "Victory at the Gates."

- Webster's Encyclopedic Dictionary of the English Language New Deluxe addition defining the word "High Places." Chapter Four- page 19 of "Victory at the Gates."

- Barclay, William (1975) The Letters to the Romans Revised addition from the daily Study Bible Series.

- Barclay, William (1975), The Letters to the Galatians and Ephesians revised edition, The Daily Study Bible Series, referencing Ephesians 6:1-20. Chapter Three - page 16 of "Victory at the Gates."

- Nelson's New Illustrated Bible Dictionary defining "Intercession." Chapter Three - page 17 of "Victory at the Gates." Defining "Wisdom." Chapter Eight – page 51 of "Victory at the Gates."

- Nelson's New Illustrated Bible Dictionary defining "High Places." Chapter Four – page 19 of "Victory at the Gates."

References

- Heidler, Robert (2007), the Second Coming of the Church. Chapter Ten pages 65, 66, 70-72 of "Victory at the Gates."

- "The Discipleship Journal," by Phil Thigpen page 115.

- Jones, Peter – Gospel Truth, Pagan Lies.

Website References

- *www.aish.com* - Chapter Five - page 28, 36, Chapter Twelve – pages 78-80 of "Victory at the Gates."

- *www.jewishsf.com* - Chapter Five – page 28, of "Victory at the Gates."

- *www.bjewsusa.com* - Chapter Five - page 29, Chapter eight – page 50 of "Victory at the Gates."

- *www.soucatdavid.israel.org* - Chapter Five – page 28 of "Victory at the Gates."

- *www.chabad.org* - Chapter Five - page 30 of "Victory at the Gates."

- *www.inner.org* - Chapter Six – page 35, Chapter Eight – page 58 and 60 of "Victory at the Gates."

- *www.templeinstitute.org* - Chapter Six –page 35-37 of "Victory at the Gates."

- *www.jhon/calendar/sivan/basics.htm* - Chapter Seven – pages 42, 43 of "Victory at the Gates."

- *www.jewfaq.org* - Chapter Nine – page 59, 61, and 62 of "Victory at the Gates."

- *www.inner.org* - Chapter Twelve and Chapter Eighteen – page 80 of "Victory at the Gates."

- *www.soucatdavid.isrealenet.org* – Chapter Five – page 28 of "Victory at the Gates."

- *www.marion institute.org* – Chapter One – page 7 of

"Victory at the Gates."

- *www.revivalhymn.com* – Chapter Three- page 18 of "Victory at the Gates."

- *www.christianity-rediscovered.blogspot.com* – Page 146 - 147 and Chapter Eighteen, "The Gate of Transformation," in "Victory at the Gates."

- *www.aboutbibleprophecy.com* – Chapter Eighteen of "Victory at the Gates."

- *www.wikipedia.org* – Chapter Eighteen of "Victory at the Gates."

- *www.programingpalace.com* – Chapter Eighteen of "Victory at the Gates."